Edwardians and Late Victorians

Edwardians and Late Victorians

ENGLISH INSTITUTE ESSAYS · 1959

EDITED WITH A FOREWORD BY *Richard Ellmann*

Columbia University Press NEW YORK AND LONDON

Foreword

The first three essays in this book are drawn from the conference on "The Last Victorians," directed by Professor George H. Ford at the session of the English Institute in 1958. The four essays that follow comprised the conference on "The Edwardians," which I directed at the 1959 session.

All the essays spring from an impatience about current interpretations of the literature written shortly before or shortly after 1900. Literary history often seems to be a struggle between books and the epithets applied to them, and sometimes epithets temporarily and unfairly vanquish books. Good works founder against some graceless label. The force of such words as "Victorian" and "modern" has pushed the intermediary period out of focus. We have been encouraged to regard the decade from 1890 to 1900 as flamboyant but basically fainthearted, while the years from 1900 to 1910 have been identified—and so lost identity —as "post-Victorian" or "pre-war."

These essays urge us to read or reread books we have grown accustomed to regard as of little consequence. Clearly the problem is different for each of the two decades. The writers of the nineties suffer from being caricatured, the Edwardians from being disregarded. There are a dozen books on the literature from 1890 to 1900, none on the literature from 1900 to 1910. So the first three essays are at pains to separate individual writers from the image of the nineties, to show that they were not just doomed and rather silly. The essayists agree that the period really begins twenty or thirty years earlier and achieves more than artistic solipsism. The next four essays, on the Edwardians, emphasize the surprising number of shared presuppositions and literary methods of this varied group.

Perhaps the principal misunderstanding of the late Victorians comes from making them simple-minded in the pursuit of art for art's sake. Mr. Hough's essay indicates, by the example of George Moore, that the quest for formal beauty went hand in hand with the desire to tell the truth about contemporary experience. Miss Temple, whose concern is with the literary critics, demonstrates that the aesthetic of the late Victorians, of Pater and others, was not a period piece but a subtle investigation of the problem of the autonomy of art, a problem which we are still investigating today. Mr. Gerber, also concerned to divorce the nineties from the disease of the same name, shows that the artistic view of experience was important to the late Victorians not because it was artistic, but because it was valid and creative. Though art for art's sake was a convenient battle cry, it was only a small part of the literary strategy of that time, and we cannot refute it by the even more banal counter-cry of ivory tower.

The essays on the Edwardians are not so much concerned to define the period in years as in reigning motives. Mr. Whitaker deals with the sudden shift in the method of W. B. Yeats at the beginning of this century, when the poet moved from verse that was visionary to verse that was dramatic. Instead of evading temporal problems, he now attempted an "agonizing and joyful" understanding and transcendence of them. History can imprison us or it can make us free, as T. S. Eliot also was to discover. Both poets moved from fear of time to its acceptance on special terms. Mr. Ray dispatches the notion that H. G. Wells had no interest in the novel as a serious form of art. Wells did not write great novels, but for fifteen years he was ambitious to write good ones. Mr. Weales's essay reveals, with Granville Barker as a striking example, that the Edwardian theater was unusually unified in its purposes and methods, which were close to the purposes and methods of the fiction and poetry of the time. The final essay specifies certain dominant attributes of the Edwardian temper as distinguished from the temper of the present day. It is clear that many of these attributes are not exclusively Edwardian—a child is bound to resemble his father— but they are formulated with a new self-consciousness in the first decade of this century.

This book does not follow to the end all the directions of inquiry to which it points. The essays in it necessarily diverge in places. But they agree in refusing to simplify, in insisting upon the intricacies which always lie behind artistic groupings. Under this inspection, the Edwardian and the late Victorian writers begin to take on an unfamiliar and therefore juster aspect.

RICHARD ELLMANN

Evanston, Illinois
January, 1960

Contents

x   *Contents*

✠

George Moore and the Nineties

GRAHAM HOUGH

I am not one who oft or much delights in contemplating the division of literary history into periods: at best it is a barren exercise. Nevertheless it has a certain importance; largely a negative importance. No doubt all history is a seamless web, and everything is continuous with everything else, and our subdivisions are imposed and arbitrary schemes. No doubt these schemes have no substantial existence, and we have no real criterion for deciding that one is right and another wrong; the most we can say is that some are appropriate and useful and others less so. The best-laid scheme cannot give us much positive assistance; but regarded simply as a heuristic mechanism an inappropriate scheme can do a good deal to deform our picture of literary history. It has seemed to me for a long time that the concept of "the Victorian age" has had just this effect. The Victorian age presumably extends from somewhere about the accession of that respectable monarch in 1837 to her death in 1901. But the life of the spirit does not coincide very accurately with the vicissitudes of the temporal power, and as a division of literary history this slice of time makes very little sense. It has presented us with the picture of an age of patient moral and social fervor on the one hand, of the slow decline of the romantic impulse on the other, both fading into a sort of penumbra after the Victorian heyday. This is succeeded by a short space of total eclipse, until the darkness is dispelled by the sudden emergence of the light of Eliot and Pound. What we have here is plainly not a very complete or accurate account of what went on, so we have been persuaded to intercalate a short period called the nineties, just to signalize our recognition of the fact that various changes were taking place. As an alternative I should like to propose for consideration a period extending from about 1880 to 1914, a period distinct in spirit from what we usually think of as Victorianism, a period in which all the foundations of modern literature were being laid, but recognizably distinct from modern literature too. I am not quite sure about 1880; a case might be made for putting the beginning of our period back into the 1870s, perhaps to the publication of Pater's *Renaissance* in 1873; but on balance 1880 is probably about right. It is not until the late seventies that the influence of Pater on style and feeling becomes decisive, or that the influence of French realism begins to make itself felt in the novel. And as for 1914—perhaps it ought to be 1910; but 1914 is such a landmark in cultural as well as political history that it seems the most appropriate point to choose.

A paper on the nineties ideally should not begin by abolishing the nineties, or by merging them in a larger unit; and one may well concede that it is in the nineties that the tendencies of the period find their fullest expression. It is the decade of the one serious poetical *cénacle,* the Rhymers' Club; of the two most characteristic literary magazines, *The Yellow Book* and *The Savoy;* of what is probably the best of the English realist novels, Moore's *Esther Waters;* and of the great social-literary scandal, the Oscar Wilde trial. But a decade is an embarrassing unit in literary history; in general it is far too short to be useful, and there is not a writer of any weight in the nineties whose significant work does not extend outside them. One has only to cite the names of James, Hardy, Conrad, Moore, Gissing, and Yeats. It is sometimes said that the nineties were not an attitude but a state of mind—a state whose peculiar color has been variously described as mauve and greenery-yallery. This is a good enough starting point for period nostalgia, a vision of the poppies and the lilies, the green nightgowns, the blue china, the gas lamps reflected in a Whistlerian Thames, the Sickert music halls, and Sherlock Holmes's Inverness cape. One may become an addict to these historic stimulants, but they do not really tell us very much. And the trouble about the actual achievements of the nineties in their most characteristic forms is that they are so minuscule. The poetry of Dowson and Lionel Johnson, Crackanthorpe's stories and Henry Harland's, will not bear very much weight. Yeats's ninetyish phase is largely proleptic—it looks forward to a much greater achievement of a different kind later on. And Wilde, except as a personality and a portent, seems to me a greatly overrated figure. So if we insist on looking at the nineties by themselves we are presented with a decade where many forces are stirring but not to any very complete purpose.

Having proposed a longer period as the appropriate unit, I should like just to suggest its general characteristics; but only in a very summary fashion, since the bare existence of these twenty-five years as a literary concept has not yet been generally recognized, still less examined. I see three principal developments. First, a greatly increased range and a new freedom in the choice of subjects from actual life; all that we ordinarily call realism. I shall not make any distinction between realism and naturalism, for though in French literary history they are always carefully distinguished, this has no particular relevance to English, and in the controversy of the 1880s the word realism is the one that seems always to have been used. Leaving aside the shocked indignation, of which there was much, we can get an idea of the cautious welcome extended to realism, and the recognition of both its novelty and its foreign origin, from Henry James's remarks on Zola:

> A novelist with a system, a passionate conviction, a great plan—incontestable attributes of M. Zola—is not now easily to be found in England or the United States, where the story-teller's art is almost exclusively feminine, is mainly in the hands of timid (even when very accomplished) women, whose acquaintance with life is severely restricted, and who are not conspicuous for general views. The novel, moreover, among ourselves, is almost always addressed to young unmarried ladies, or at least always assumes them to be a large part of the novelist's public.
>
> This fact, to a French story-teller, appears, of course, a damnable restriction. . . . Half of life is a sealed book to young unmarried ladies, and how can a novel be worth anything that deals with only half of life? These objections are perfectly valid, and it may be said that our English system is a good thing for virgins and boys, and a bad thing for the

novel itself, when the novel is regarded as something more than a simple *jeu d'esprit,* and considered as a composition that treats of life at large and helps us to *know.*

I take this quotation from an advertisement for the series of translations of Zola published by Vizetelly from 1884 onwards. Vizetelly was, of course, the publisher who was most closely associated with the realist movement; he was prosecuted for his publications and eventually imprisoned, in 1888. In subsequent comment on the affair he is generally represented as a sort of martyr for culture, but a further perusal of the advertisement pages I am speaking of leads one to take this with just a small pinch of salt. It may be that Vizetelly was filled only with a pure desire to serve modern letters and to show contemporary society the realities on which it was based, but it is also fairly evident that Vizetelly's Realistic Novels are advertised with half an eye towards a possibly scandalous success; and I mention this because the suggestion that "This is not for young ladies" (or the alternative suggestion that "This will certainly be read by young ladies but their parents ought not to know"), made seriously, or defiantly, or with a behind-the-hand snigger, is a very recognizable element in the literature of this time, quite as recognizable as the high Victorian attitude of Tennyson—

> The prudent partner of his blood
> Lean'd on him, faithful, gentle, good,
> Wearing the rose of womanhood—

and so forth. The advertisement of George Moore's *A Mummer's Wife,* for example, begins with the announcement: "This book has been placed in the Index Expurgatorius of the Select Circulating Libraries of Messrs. Mudie and W. H. Smith and Son."

The second development is a confused set of tendencies that cluster round the notion of art for art's sake. These never amount to a formal doctrine in England, and they hold together in a loose synthesis a number of different ideas, mostly derived from France. Parnassians, symbolists, decadents—these school labels have a tolerably plain meaning in French literary history, but English literary ideas are much less clearly analyzed. Art for art's sake, for what the phrase is worth, goes back to Gautier, and Gautier had been an influence on Swinburne in the 1860s. Transposed into a moral rather than a literary code, it reappears in the preface to Pater's *Renaissance;* and the cult of exquisite sensations, expressed in the languid Paterian rhythms, haunts the production of the nineties and extends some considerable distance into this century. But the strictly literary ideals to which it gave rise remain shifting and uncertain. On the one hand we are constantly hearing echoes of "L'Art," the last poem in *Émaux et Camées,* with its praise of a hard-chiseled perfection of form:

> Lutte avec le carrare,
> Avec le paros dur
>   Et rare,
> Gardiens du contour pur;
>
> Peintre, fuis l'aquarelle,
> Et fixe la couleur
>   Trop frêle
> Au four de l'émailleur.

On the other hand, the quite contrary doctrine of Verlaine's "Art Poètique":

Il faut aussi que tu n'ailles point
Choisir tes mots sans quelque méprise:
Rien de plus cher que la chanson grise
Ou l'Indécis au Précis se joint.

Car nous voulons la Nuance encore,
Pas la Couleur, rien que la Nuance!

So that we are left uncertain whether the prevalent ideal is an intaglio cut in the hardest stone or a misty Whistler nocturne. But what these ideals have in common is an insistence on the claims as the artist as artificer against those of the artist as interpreter of life. "The Yellow Dwarf," the pseudonymous book reviewer of *The Yellow Book* (his name, by the way, is borrowed from *Le Nain Jaune,* a Parnassian periodical of the 1860s), makes a great point of the purely aesthetic nature of his criticism, and he is greatly disturbed when he suspects that a work of fiction might have a moral or be intended as a tract for the times. And, as in France, this lightweight aestheticism passes over into symbolism. Whether there is anything in English letters that can be called a symbolist movement I am not sure; but the word seems inevitable, and is not without its uses. Symbolism can be said to occur when the cult of the exquisite, particular sensation, embodied in the perfect form, begins to acquire transcendental overtones, begins to be seen as a means of access to a more authentic world underlying the world of appearances. As a half-sentimental literary idea we see this floating around in a good many places. As a serious conviction, involving the whole moral and literary personality, we see it in the early essays of Yeats.

Now these two tendencies, the realist and the symbolist-aesthetic, are inveterately opposed in France. But in England they show a curious tendency to fuse together. This is because moral ideas in England are commonly clearer and more strongly held than literary ones; a literary controversy tends to shift itself to the moral plane. And morally the two different schools are in façt moving in the same direction. Both place the demands of art outside and above moral exigencies, and the need for a moral emancipation is so much more pressing in England that it obscures other differences. The movement may be towards fantasy and dream, or it may be towards the recognition of the most sordid social actualities; but these do not feel themselves to be vitally opposed, for they are both expressions of the same need. Moral and psychological adventurousness and the pursuit of an exquisite and refined form go hand in hand in England, and even tend to be seen as much the same thing. George Eliot, we may notice, comes in for equally heavy knocks on both counts —for lumbering bluntness of style and form, and for the ever-present moral superintendence under which her work is seen to labor.

The third very marked feature of the time is a conscious reaction against the English literary tradition. This is something relatively new, at any rate since neo-classical times. It formed no part of the romantic upheaval, though I suppose a foretaste of it may be found in Matthew Arnold's exhortations against English provincialism and complacency. But the reaction I am speaking of has a new flavor, and it continues into the most formative literature of the next decades. It is the beginning of that chronic Francophilia that affects many of the Anglo-American intelligentsia even to our own day. The manifestations that first leap to the mind are the slightly absurd ones—Pater murmuring that Poe was so coarse, he could only read him in Baudelaire's translation; Wilde writing *Salomé* in not very good French; the scraps of French idiom that interlard the pages of Henry James—down to the still current illusions that French coffee is good and the architecture of Paris beautiful. Of course the influence of France was necessary; it was the only one possible. It was an example of that perpetual process of fruitful interchange of which the history of European letters is composed. But there was in this particular wave of French influence an element of affectation. Yeats's use of Mallarmé—whom he cannot possibly have understood—as a name to conjure with provides us with one instance. There went with it a slightly perverse determination to throw overboard some of the most characteristic achievements of the English genius—Moore's dismissal of Shakespeare and the traditional English novel, for example. Without the slightest leaning to that absurdest of attitudes, a literary nationalism, it remains true that the actual achieved body of work in a given language is an inescapable condition for future work. The nineties show signs of wishing to make an escape; and, though this is another subject, and complicated by Anglo-American literary relations, the tendency persisted into the *avant garde* of the twentieth century.

In a period where many of the representative writings are on a very small scale it is difficult to find a typical figure to stand for the central movement of the time. I have a candidate to propose for this office; it is George Moore. There is no particular virtue in being typical; but even if it is the portrait of an age that we are trying to draw there are advantages in examining an individual man, an actual writer, rather than tendencies exhibited in fragments. George Moore has some qualifications that are particularly useful to us in this respect. In the first place, he exists. He is discernible with the naked eye, which can hardly be said for Crackanthorpe or Dowson. Never quite in the center of the picture, he nevertheless played a real part in the literary history of the *fin de siècle,* and in his vivid, outrageous autobiography he has played a considerable part in chronicling it. He has a large body of work to his credit, uneven it is true, but some of it of undeniable excellence, and much of it of peculiar interest. And although his career extends far into this century, he remained remarkably faithful to the intuitions of his earlier years. Even his defects are for our present purpose a recommendation. Moore was not Prince Hamlet, nor was meant to be; almost at times the fool. He was incapable of what in any ordinary acceptation of the term would be called thought. He picks up ideas from everywhere, never understands them quite thoroughly or thinks them out, mixes them up to make a miscellaneous stew, and often pretends to knowledge that he does not really possess. As an informant on matters of fact he is unreliable in the extreme. To anyone attempting a critical examination of Moore, particularly to anyone who is sensible of his merits, these are highly embarrassing qualities. But if we want to feel the form and pressure of the time they are extremely useful ones. He wrote of himself:

> My soul, so far as I understand it, has very kindly taken colour and form from the many various modes of life that self-will and an impetuous temperament have forced me to indulge in. Therefore I may say that I am free from original

qualities, defects, tastes, etc. . . . I came into the world apparently with a nature like a smooth sheet of wax, bearing no impress but capable of receiving any; of being moulded into all shapes.

And it is so with his literary development too; he picks up like a magpie all the notions and influences at large in the world around him, spills them out with an air of proud discovery—in fact, as Oscar Wilde said to him, conducts his education in public. If we want to find out what the literary scene looked like to a young man of advanced tastes in the eighties and nineties we can hardly do better than look at his early works. Greater literary personalities will tell us less. The tireless spiritual energy of Yeats, the quick-witted positiveness of Shaw, are too idiosyncratic to tell us much except about their possessors.

The document I wish to look at is the *Confessions of a Young Man*. It was written in 1886; it refers to a period between 1873, when Moore first went to Paris, and 1883, when his first novel appeared; and as we now have it, it was annotated by its author at two later dates. I remember abominating it when I first read it, years ago; and it does indeed give the picture of an intolerable young coxcomb. But I entirely failed to see its significance. It is an account of Moore's literary education, and pretty well the complete account, since he was almost illiterate when he first went to France. It is an education picked up in cafés and studios, the editorial offices of magazines, and the Gaiety bar. We need not stickle for the factual accuracy of the story. The apartment with the red drawing-room, the Buddha, the python, and the Turkish couches is unlikely to have been as Moore describes it in the mid-1870s. It seems to owe far too much to Huysmans's

A Rebours. And *A Rebours* did not come out till 1884. What we are contemplating in fact is a panoramic view of the formation of a taste and an attitude, of all the varied aesthetic and social influences that went to make it, from the standpoint of 1886. It is a view that still seemed valid to Moore in 1904, and even beyond the limits of our period, in 1916.

The inevitable first reaction to the book is to find it an appalling muddle. Enthusiasms and recantations seem to follow each other in no sort of order. Every opinion is contradicted by its opposite a few pages farther on. There are no dates, and no possibility of making the story into an intelligible chronological sequence. Then one realizes that Moore is perfectly well aware of this and has even made his capriciousness into a sort of principle. "Never could I interest myself in a book," he writes, "if it were not the exact diet my mind required at the time, or in the very immediate future." And later, in excusing himself for lack of sensibility to Shakespeare, "There are affinities in literature corresponding to, and very analogous to, sexual affinities—the same unreasoned attractions, the same pleasures, the same lassitudes. Those we have loved most we are most indifferent to. Shelley, Gautier, Zola, Flaubert, Goncourt! how I have loved you all; and now I could not, would not, read you again." But there are other ways of revealing a sensibility and an attitude than the ordered chronological *Bildungsroman*. This pell-mell jumble of passions and revulsions spreads out, as it were, the contents of Moore's imagination for our inspection; and we can see that the objects displayed, apparently a mere chance assortment, actually fall into two groups. One group is composed of fantasies and dreams, often slightly perverse fantasies and dreams, unchecked by bourgeois ethics or ordinary social reality. The other group consists of equally passionate aspirations after the actualities of life, the tangible realities of contemporary experience and modern urban living. These two enthusiasms sometimes clash violently. Each at times tries to deny the existence of the other, yet both continue to exist—and even in the end come to a kind of reconciliation. They are united, not only as the most staring opposites may be, by the accident of inhering in the same personality, but by a real common factor. The common element is the purely literary one, the need that each passion has to find its fullest and justest verbal expression. Starting with a notable ignorance of both English grammar and the English vocabulary, Moore ultimately finds the ruling passion of his life in the desire to write well.

Fantasy and dream came first, and came even at first in a verbal embodiment. His first literary passion was for the mere name of a novel he heard his parents discussing—*Lady Audley's Secret*. This was followed by the revelation of Shelley, also turned to initially for the same reason. "Lady Audley! What a beautiful name! . . . Shelley! That crystal name, and his poetry also crystalline." Most of the English lyric poets were read soon after. But from Shelley the young Moore had learnt atheism, and he followed this up by a course of the rationalist classics, Lecky and Buckle. It is noticeable that George Eliot comes in with these. She appears as the great agnostic, not as an artist; and the only one of the classic English novelists that Moore mentions with any enthusiasm is Dickens. Then to France, to study painting; not that he had any talent, but France and art became the objects of a romantic devotion, like the names of Lady Audley and

Shelley. There were some flirtations with Hugo and Musset; but the first real revelation came from Gautier, from reading *Mademoiselle de Maupin*. It would be hard to exaggerate the influence of this work on the sensibility of the *fin de siècle* in England. It is constantly cited and referred to; and still more often its situations and its spirit are echoed without open acknowledgement. Both his own panegyrics and later scholarship have shown how decisive was the influence of Gautier on Swinburne; and Moore was sufficiently acute to notice it himself. "The 'Hymn to Proserpine' and 'Dolores' are wonderful lyrical versions of Mlle de Maupin," he writes. The frank sensuality, the delight in visible and tangible beauty, combined with the unquiet romantic *Sehnsucht,* the longing for an ideal satisfaction, was a combination of ingredients that the more decorous English romanticism had never supplied. Above all there was the hint of perversity brought in by the epicene nature of the hero-heroine; a double delight, for it was at once a new source of erotic stimulation and a new means to *épater le bourgeois*. Moore expresses the spirit in which it was accepted with uncommon clarity:

> I read "Mlle de Maupin" at a moment when I was weary of spiritual passion, and this great exaltation of the visible above the invisible at once conquered and led me captive. This plain scorn of a world exemplified in lacerated saints and a crucified Redeemer opened up a prospect of new beliefs and new joys in things and new revolts against all that had come to form part and parcel of the commonalty of mankind. Shelley's teaching had been, while accepting the body, to dream of the soul as a star, and so preserve our ideal;

but now I saw suddenly, with delightful clearness and in-
toxicating conviction that by looking without shame and
accepting with love the flesh, I might raise it to as high a
place within as divine a light as ever the soul had been set in.

It was above all the tone of *Mademoiselle de Maupin* that
Moore picked up, and it is a tone that is to echo through much
of the literature of the nineties and to give it much of its peculiar
flavor. It is a young man's tone, and that of a young man whom
our elders would certainly have called a cad. It is rather light-
heartedly erotic, and quite openly predatory. It is haunted by
sexuality and makes a great deal of its "paganism," yet it does
not for a moment suggest the antique world; rather a setting of
deuxième empire frou-frou, tea-roses, Parma violets, the minor
pleasures of an elegant nineteenth-century Bohemianism. Yet
beneath this worldly assurance the note of romantic idealism is
never quite absent; the young social and sexual buccaneer is
haunted by the ghost of a sad Pierrot sighing after an impossible
love. Let us look at a few examples.

> Why should I undertake to keep a woman by me for the
> entire space of her life, watching her grow fat, grey, wrinkled
> and foolish? Think of the annoyance of perpetually looking
> after any one, especially a woman! Besides, marriage is an-
> tagonistic to my ideal.   (Moore, *Confessions*)

> If I were to be the lover of one of these ladies like a pale
> narcissus, moist with a tepid dew of tears, and bending
> with willowy languor over the new marble tomb of a spouse,
> happily and recently defunct, I should be as wretched as the
> dear departed was in his lifetime.   (Gautier, *Maupin*)

He can read through the slim woman whose black hair, a-glitter with diamonds, contrasts with her white satin; an old man is talking to her, she dances with him, and she refused a young man a moment before. This is a bad sign, our Lovelace knows it; there is a stout woman of thirty-five, who is looking at him, red satin bodice, doubtful taste. He looks away; a little blonde woman fixes her eyes on him, she looks as innocent as a child; instinctively our Lovelace turns to his host. "Who is that little blonde woman over there, the right-hand corner?" he asks. "Ah, that is Lady ——." "Will you introduce me?" "Certainly." Lovelace has made up his mind.   (Moore, *Confessions*)

All this does not prevent me from positively wanting a mistress. I do not know who she will be, but among the women of my acquaintance I see nobody who could suitably fill this dignified position. Those who may be regarded as young enough are wanting in beauty or intellectual charm; those who are beautiful and young are basely and forbiddingly virtuous, or lack the necessary freedom; and then there is always some husband, some brother, a mother or an aunt, somebody or other, with prying eyes and large ears, who must either be cajoled or given short shrift.

(Gautier, *Maupin*)

I was absorbed in the life of woman—the mystery of petticoats, so different from the staidness of trousers! the rolls of hair entwined with so much art, and suggesting so much colour and perfume, so different from the bare crop; the unnaturalness of the waist in stays! plenitude and slenderness of silk. . . . A world of calm colour with phantoms moving, floating past and changing in dim light—an averted face with abundant hair, the gleam of a perfect bust or the poise of a neck turning slowly round, the gaze of deep trans-lucid eyes. I loved women too much to give myself wholly to one.   (Moore, *Confessions*)

It makes me have a low opinion of women when I see how infatuated they often are with blackguards who despise and deceive them, instead of taking a lover—some staunch and sincere young man who would consider himself very lucky, and would simply worship them; I myself, for example, am such a one. It is true that men of the former kind abound in the drawing-rooms, where they preen themselves for all to behold, and are always lounging on the back of some settee, while I remain at home, my forehead pressed against the window-pane, watching the river shroud itself in haze and the mists rising, while silently setting up in my heart the scented shrine, the peerless temple, in which I am to install the future idol of my soul.   (Gautier, *Maupin*)

I have two points to make in setting these extracts side by side. One is how extraordinarily closely Moore echoes Gautier's tone, and how easy it is to recognize that tone as particularly char-acteristic of the nineties. We find it again and again in Wilde, in *The Yellow Book* and *The Savoy,* and even, though decorously veiled and entirely without the connivance of the author, in some of the characters of Henry James. The second point is that the attitudes implied here are entirely social and sexual. But *Made-moiselle de Maupin* had a preface—the famous preface which was the manifesto of the art-for-art's-sake movement. Moore does not mention it, but we can hardly suppose that he did not read it. And we later find, by a curious linkage, that he associates *Mademoiselle de Maupin* with Pater's *Marius the Epicurean*. There seems to be little in common between the aesthetic sensuality of Gautier and the spiritualized hedonism of Pater. It may of course be that the one is simply the Oxford version of the other, and Moore partly makes the association on those grounds —with a certain rude psychological insight and a good deal of injustice to what Pater supposed himself to be saying.

Mr. Pater can join hands with Gautier in saying

> je trouve la terre aussi belle que le ciel, et je pense que la correction de la forme est la vertu.

"I think that correctness of form is virtue"; that is the real link that Moore makes between Gautier and Pater. The social and sexual antinomianism is only the correlative of a general pursuit of formal beauty, which can manifest itself as much in the sphere of verbal arrangement as in the sphere of conduct.

> But "Marius the Epicurean" was more to me than a mere emotional influence, precious and rare though that may be, for this book was the first in English prose I had come across that procured for me any genuine pleasure in the language itself, in the combination of words for silver or gold chime, and unconventional cadence, and for all those lurking half-meanings, and that evanescent suggestion, like the odour of dead roses, that words retain to the last of other times and elder usage. . . . "Marius" was the stepping-stone that carried me across the channel into the genius of my own tongue.

I said before that psychological adventurousness and the search for perfection of form go hand in hand. Here we see the process in action. Gautier suggests a style of life; Pater extends it; and at the same time he suggests a style of writing. The cultivation of a mannered exquisiteness of sensation leads directly into the cultivation of prose as a deliberate aesthetic instrument.

After the reading of *Maupin* Moore plunged deep into the waters of aestheticism. Other tales of Gautier followed, and the delicately chiseled nostalgias of *Emaux et Camées*. The inevitable next step was Baudelaire.

> No longer is it the grand barbaric face of Gautier; now it is the clean-shaven face of the mock priest, the slow, cold eye, and the sharp, cunning sneer of the cynical libertine who will be tempted that he may better know the worthlessness of temptation. "Les Fleurs du Mal," beautiful flowers, beautiful in sublime decay. What a great record is yours, and were Hell a reality how many souls would we find wreathed with your poisonous blossoms.

(There is no need to suppose that Moore in 1886 wrote these lines without a tinge of irony.) Bertrand's *Gaspard de la Nuit;* Villiers de l'Isle Adam, whom Moore used to meet at the Nouvelle Athènes; Verlaine; Gustave Kahn's experiments in *vers libre* and faint evocative vocabulary; Ghil's theory of colored vowels, a development of the doctrine of Rimbaud's sonnet, which gave rise to an often quoted passage in *Muslin;* Mallarmé, whose conversation Moore enjoyed, while confessing that he was quite unable to understand either the poetry or the Symbolist theory. Excited by this heady brew, it is not surprising that Moore was unable to appreciate the contemporary experiments in the poetry of common life. When he came to read Coppée he was able to enjoy only his early Parnassian poems.

> But the exquisite perceptivity Coppée showed in his modern poems, the certainty with which he raised the commonest subject, investing it with sufficient dignity for his purpose, escaped me wholly, and I could not but turn with horror from such poems as "La Nourrice" and "Le Petit Epicier." I could not understand how anybody could bring himself to acknowledge the vulgar details of our vulgar age.

But a new force was piling up behind the aesthetic screen, and it was soon to burst out. Moore was busy trying to write short stories apparently in the manner of Villiers' *Contes Cruels,* and poems, "Roses of Midnight," in what he believed to be the manner of Baudelaire. One day by chance he read in a magazine an article by Zola (presumably *Le Roman Experimental*). The words *naturalisme, la verité, la science* affronted his eyes. He learnt that one should write with as little imagination as possible, that contrived plot in a novel or a play was illiterate and puerile. It all struck him as a revelation, and he realized the sterile eccentricity of his own aestheticism. He had read a few chapters of *L'Assommoir* when it had appeared in serial form, but like others of his tastes had dismissed it as an absurdity. Now he began to buy up the back numbers of the *Voltaire,* the weekly in which Zola was making propaganda for the naturalist cause.

> The idea of a new art based on science, in opposition to the art of the old world that was based on the imagination, an

art that should explain all things and embrace modern life in its entirety, in its endless ramifications, be, as it were, a new creed in a new civilisation, filled me with wonder, and I stood dumb before the vastness of the conception, and the towering height of the ambition.

This mood of enraptured stupefaction did not last; at the time of writing the *Confessions,* in 1886, he is able to look back at the Zola articles and say "Only the simple crude statements of a man of powerful mind, but singularly narrow vision." And a few pages farther on from the account of the naturalist revelation is a thoroughgoing attack on Zola's limitations, an attack whose consequences are amusingly described in the essay "A Visit to Médan." But it is not my purpose to write the history of Moore's literary opinions in detail. The point is that from now on the idea of a distinctively modern art, grounding itself on the realities of the contemporary world, lies side by side with aesthetic fantasy in Moore's mind. It is surprising how easily they came to lie side by side. On a later page of the *Confessions, Mademoiselle de Maupin* and *L'Assommoir* are cited together as the two books above all from which the respectable circulating-library young lady must turn away; they are mentioned almost as though they were the twin pillars of modern letters, in spite of the fact that *Maupin* had appeared in 1836, and that the two works had nothing whatever in common, except that neither is exactly the thing *à mettre entre les mains de toute jeune fille.* And the fact is that naturalism did not drive out aestheticism, it substituted a new aestheticism of an extended kind. The immediate effect of the Zola discovery was to send Moore back to Coppée's modern poems, and to persuade him to modernize his "Roses of Midnight." But this soon proved to be a hopeless enterprise, and he turns to reflect, not at all on the social and descriptive implications of naturalism, but on its purely literary qualities. He rereads *L'Assommoir* and is impressed by its "strength, height and decorative grandeur," by the "immense harmonic development of the idea, and the fugal treatment of the different scenes," by "the lordly, river-like roll of the narrative." In short, it was "the idea of the new aestheticism—the new art corresponding to modern, as ancient art corresponded to ancient life" that captivated him and was to compel his imagination for many years to come.

The later history of Zola's reputation has borne out Moore's intuition. Towards the end of the *Confessions* he writes:

> One thing that cannot be denied to the realists: a constant and intense desire to write well, to write artistically. When I think of what they have done in the matter of the use of words, of the myriad verbal effects they have discovered, of the thousand forms of composition they have created, how they have remodelled and refashioned the language in their untiring striving for intensity of expression, for the very osmazome of art, I am lost in ultimate wonder and admiration. What Hugo did for French verse, Flaubert, Goncourt, Zola, and Huysmans have done for French prose.

It would once have seemed eccentric to talk of Zola in this way, perhaps did even when Moore was writing. But in later years nobody has been very interested in Zola the reporter and sociologist; and complaints about the supposed coarseness and crudity of his style have given way, and justly, to admiration for his impressionist painting and the organization of his large set pieces. The massive symbolism in his writing has not passed unnoticed, and the flat opposition between naturalist and symbolist has been much played down. By now, when the professed "scientific" pretensions of *Le Roman Experimental* can no longer be taken seriously, the real nature of Zola's achievement can be seen more clearly, and it is seen much as Moore saw it. In making the transition from Zola's untenable naturalist theory to his far more interesting and comprehensive practice Moore is taking the line that both criticism and fiction itself were to take in the years to come.

But Moore's discipleship to Zola was brief. He soon saw something nearer to his real aim in Flaubert, where the demands of a scrupulous realism are united with an equal scrupulosity of rhythm and phrasing. However great the difference between their achievements, Flaubert's strict attachment to the truth, to be sought only through formal perfection, probably came nearest to embodying Moore's artistic ideal. *A Mummer's Wife* is his only Zolaesque novel; he was annoyed if one did not recognize that *Esther Waters* was in inspiration "pure Flaubert." But strangely, even Flaubert was not the object of Moore's lasting devotion. Talking of his own literary infidelities he says "even a light of love is constant, if not faithful, to her *amant de coeur"*; and the most enduring of his literary passions was for Balzac. "Upon that rock I built my church, and his great and valid talent saved me from the shoaling waters of new aestheticisms, the putrid mud of naturalism, and the faint and sickly surf of the symbolists." It is only in Balzac that he can find an unrestricted romantic imagination united with a complete engagement in the involved turmoil of contemporary life. Essentially a spectator on the sidelines, Moore is fascinated by that colossal vitality; and if for Alisander he is more than a little o'erparted, we can at least recognize in the totality of his work something of his master's passion for the diversity of human experience.

Disorderly and capricious as Moore's expression of his enthusiasms is, it can still tell us something, and something that is of importance beyond his own career. He was more completely involved in French literature than any other writer of the nineties —more even than Symons; and we can see in him a complete microcosm of the French influences that were then reshaping English literature. His experience tells us of the opening of a new chapter in the history of English fiction. Three steady preoccupations can be discerned among his shifting allegiances: one is with telling the truth about experience instead of merely devising an agreeable story; the second is with imaginative freedom in spite of the circulating libraries and the young ladies; the third is with formal justness and beauty in expression and organization, instead of the labored or slapdash approximations to which the English novel in all but its highest moments had been prone. Together they make a break with many of the traditions of English fiction—with the traditions of picaresque adventure, indiscriminate humor, genial satire, and reforming zeal. A severer artistic ideal takes their place. And this break is not merely a matter of Moore's own work. We are not considering his intrinsic quality at the moment, though my own conviction is that it is far higher than has been generally recognized; we are using him simply as a convenient periscope to survey the literary scene of his time. And the lessons he was learning were also being learnt, wholly or in part, by Hardy, Conrad, and Henry James.

James is a far greater, Hardy and Conrad more central writers than Moore. It is relatively easy to fit them into a "great tradition" of English fiction. Moore has always his own marked idiosyncrasy, and the criticism of our time, in its preoccupation with prevalent trends and successful revolutions rather than with individual quality, has been inclined to see it as a dead end. This is not, I think, true; and if it is necessary to justify Moore to the trend-mongers one may do so by showing that he was leading, if not up the main road, into an area where the greatest prose experiment of our time has its beginning. We have seen Moore oscillating between aesthetic reverie and realism, and if we were to follow the development of his art we should find him in the end arriving at a style that was to harmonize the two. He manages in his best work to present in all their uncompromising contingency the actualities of common experience, and yet to preserve the inevitability of impression, the delicate rightness of diction and rhythm that he had learned from the high priests of a scrupulous art. At the end of our period, when Moore was past the threshold of old age, another Irish writer brought out his youthful confessions; and in it he defined the function of the poet, the literary artist, as it appeared to his eyes. It is to be "the mediator between the world of reality and the world of dreams." No writer in any age has carried farther than James Joyce the dual allegiance to an exhaustive naturalism on the one hand and a complex aesthetic symbolism on the other; and I think it is likely that neither the title nor the content of Joyce's *Portrait of the Artist as a Young Man* would have been quite the same in

1916 if it had not been for the prior existence of Moore's *Confessions of a Young Man* in 1886. And there are other resemblances more strongly marked. Critics have often spoken about the absolute originality of Joyce's *Dubliners;* and that is a curious instance of how far George Moore's achievements have dropped out of sight—itself perhaps a curious instance of the general failure to recognize the importance of the *fin de siècle* as a formative power in modern literature. For *Dubliners* has an obvious ancestor in Moore's stories in *The Untilled Field.* Joyce's stories have an urban instead of a rural setting, and make far more use of the romantic-ironical contrast. But it is surprising that the closeness of his manner to Moore's has not been observed. Part of it no doubt is a matter of a common discipleship. Moore's debt to Pater's prose has always been acknowledged; and Joyce's use of the same master is obvious, especially in *Portrait of the Artist.* It would be too long to illustrate in detail, but the echoed cadences sometimes reveal themselves in a sentence.

> From without as from within the waters had flowed over his barriers: their tides once more began to jostle fiercely above the crumbled mole.   (Joyce, *Portrait of the Artist*)
>
> I could see that he believed the story, and for the moment I, too, believed in an outcast Venus becoming the evil spirit of a village that would not accept her as divine.
>
> (Moore, *The Untilled Field*)

Neither of these dying falls would be quite as they are if they had not echoed so often already through Pater's prose. In feeling and treatment too we can see common obligations. "The Window" in *The Untilled Field* and "Clay" in *Dubliners* are both stories about humble old women; and I doubt whether either of them would exist if Flaubert had not written "Un Coeur Simple." But the similarities between the two volumes are so marked and pervasive that I am persuaded the debt is more direct. Moore said later that he began *The Untilled Field* "with the hope of furnishing the young Irish of the future with models"; and reading *Dubliners* beside the earlier book we can hardly doubt that for Joyce he achieved just that. He also said that, as the work progressed, "the first stories begot a desire to paint the portrait of my country"; almost the words in which Joyce described to his publisher the purpose of *Dubliners:* "to write a chapter of the moral history of my country." One could go on to speak of the last story in *Dubliners,* "The Dead," and of how extraordinarily close it is in feeling to, say, "The Exile" and "Home Sickness" in Moore's collection. But to do justice to the charity, the gentleness, the centrality of feeling that these two lonely antinomian writers achieve in these beautiful tales would be to desert periods and influences, and would demand quite other tools and another manner. I end on this note just to give a small illustration of what is still often forgotton—how intimate the connection is between the writing of the late nineteenth century and what is most new and living in the twentieth.

The Ivory Tower as Lighthouse

RUTH Z. TEMPLE

The metaphor I have chosen for my title gives my case away at the outset, so there is no use trying to lead you insensibly to share my conclusion before I have reached it. Moreover, I have already committed both metaphor and conclusion to print. If I revert to the figure here, that is because I find it amply sustained by the fresh evidence I have accumulated in a further consideration of the criticism of the nineties. And, what is even more reassuring, the conclusion is now enunciated here and there by voices more persuasive than my own.

My strategy, then, will be to present my argument baldly and boldly, if not to induce assent, at least to provoke controversy. If I claim too much, I must protest as my excuse that others have claimed too little. I contend that the criticism of the nineties stands up very well on comparison with either Victorian criticism or contemporary criticism in England and America. And I contend that the best criticism of the nineties was that called "aesthetic." [1] But before proceeding to the critics and their ideas I must deal with some of the difficulties raised by conventional terminology and chronology. What does "Victorian" mean, and how and when did the Victorian period generate aestheticism?

The Victorian period has been undergoing "reappraisal" recently and the official effort of the MLA on this topic (*The Reinterpretation of Victorian Literature,* 1950) exhibits a disturbing lack of agreement as to its dates. Norman Foerster thinks the period should not be called Victorian because it ended in 1880, that is, more than two decades before the end of the reign. Another of the essayists, attempting to prove that Victorian England was cosmopolitan, uses for evidence authors and attitudes of the 1880s and 1890s. The most helpful remark I find in this rather unsatisfactory book is the editor's (J. E. Baker), that if there had not been a dearth of great books from 1825 to 1835 we should now be treating the whole nineteenth century as a unit at least as homogeneous as the neo-classical period.[2] What an advantage this would have been. We should then have been spared the term Victorian, surely one of the most peculiar in literary terminology.[3] (According to the *NED* it was a late Victorian who conferred this distinction upon the reigning monarch—a lady innocent of interest in the arts, who managed, someone has said, her kingdom like her kitchen.) And we should also have been spared the trouble of making out a case for "Great Victorians" as equals of the "Great Romantics" but somehow *not* romantics in order that we might have matching courses in the two "halves" of the nineteenth century.

Terminology is compelling, and the lack of parallelism in our names for the two divisions of the century has confused the history of literature in the nineteenth century and obscured its analogy with that of the eighteenth century.[4] Just before the eighteenth century begins, a great critic who is also a poet lays down certain principles (by no means entirely new and mostly from France) and illustrates them. In the first half of the century these principles are generally operative in the work of the leading writers and continue to have, as it were, currency and official weight even until the century ends; but well before 1750 new ideas and forms begin to contest the field with the established ones, and gradually the new ones assume dominance. In the nineteenth century the case is less simple in the measure that romanticism is by definition more various than classicism. Yet Wordsworth takes the place of Dryden, and the currents which have coursed through the preceding epoch (some from Germany and France, some native) find distinguished expositors in Coleridge, Byron, Shelley, Keats, and Scott. After 1830 these currents are modified in their direction and expression by new ideas and forms: from science, from abroad (France and then Norway and Russia). As classicism gave way before romanticism, so early romanticism gives way to its progeny: realism, naturalism, impressionism, symbolism. Each age is an age that is dying *and* one that is coming to birth. The "great" Victorians and some of the lesser ones are the continuators of romanticism, which has lost its first fine careless rapture. Those who prepare the new age, our own, are almost without exception the ones who feel the force of the new, especially the movements in French art. The nineties, then, is not a decade set apart and hedged about. It takes its place —a culminating one—in the setting of the tide toward the twentieth century.[5]

This is all sufficiently obvious, but it may need saying to counteract certain vulgar errors in literary history and criticism, such as, that the aesthetic movement was a comedy of errors,[6] or that Tennyson and Browning were the new poets of their age (they were rather the representatives of a declining tradition—and as such could be popular poets as Shelley and Keats had not been— the *new* poets were Meredith and Hardy). The second half of the nineteenth century, like the second half of the eighteenth, was not a great period in English art, but in both periods the new criticism was one of the most effective intellectual enter- prises and helped to lay the foundation for the next age.

I have not gone this long way around to deprecate the term Victorian and in a sense to deprecate what is known as Vic- torian literature only to get the nineties on higher ground. I be- lieve this *is* the result; if the Victorian age is exalted there is bound to be a dip before we reach the twin pinnacle of the twen- tieth century or, some might say, before the nineties engage us on the slide to Avernus down which we are still coasting. My purpose, however, was other, and twofold. First, to point out the difficulty of fair appraisal of any aspect of the nineteenth century when the whole is thrown out of focus by a misleading division. And, second, to prepare the way for notice that I shall not limit my subsequent remarks to what happened between 1890 and 1900. As the new movements were well under way by the 1870s, it will be necessary to take a more comprehensive view.

Indeed it will be necessary to talk about Pater. Although the two books of his which most influenced the nineties were pub- lished in the two preceding decades, he is the definer of the aesthetic critic and the impressionist method. My chief interest is not historical but theoretical, and I am concerned to say some- thing about the meaning of the words and phrases which are so generally used to justify for the nineties the designation *fin de siècle* or *decadent*. My strictly nineties' examples will be Wilde, Moore, and Arthur Symons. Since Moore is the subject of another paper in the series I shall mention him briefly and only because he fills a gap in my argument. On Symons I shall be brief, too, partly for reasons of time and partly because I can only repeat what I have said more fully elsewhere. Moreover the much needed reassessment of Symons has begun with the chapter on him in Frank Kermode's illuminating book, *Romantic Image* (London [1951]).

In order to advance my contention that we owe much to the post-Victorians I shall introduce into my remarks on Pater, the godfather of the nineties, certain comparisons with Arnold, a Victorian—though these two were of course contemporaries.

Arnold is the most noted (though not necessarily the most noteworthy) critic of the later nineteenth century. Arnold's stock is very high today; Pater's very low. Arnold is continually the subject of almost uniformly adulatory essays; Pater of almost none—excepting the admirable chapter in Mr. Hough's book, *The Last Romantics* (London [1949]), and a study which has just appeared of his style.[7] (I hope these may be portents.) Though in informed quarters some doubt is cast on Arnold's value as *literary* critic, he is still generally supposed to have been what he demonstrably was not: that is, a knowledgeable and useful intermediary between French literature and the English reading public, a clear and consistent thinker, a learned man, and an urbane stylist. Pater, though his contemporaries regarded him so highly, is today on the low ground of the aesthetic movement for which he provided the watchwords and the critical method (or,

as Gaunt puts it, he was "the original aesthete and fifth columnist
. . . of the aesthetic invasion"[8]). Eliot's essay on Arnold and
Pater links the two in this way: " 'Art for art's sake' is the off-
spring of Arnold's Culture; and we can hardly venture to say that
it is even a perversion of Arnold's doctrine, considering how very
vague and ambiguous that doctrine is." It is to Pater's credit, Eliot
thinks, that whereas Arnold Hellenized and Hebraized by turns,
Pater only Hellenized. But Eliot writes Pater off as literary critic,
for "being primarily a moralist, he was incapable of seeing any
work of art simply as it is."[9] That the moralist cannot be an
impartial literary critic is quite an admission for Mr. Eliot to
make, and one is a little surprised to find Pater's rather than
Arnold's name in that sentence. However, it is standard practice
to rehabilitate Pater by proving that, since he was inconsistent, he
did not mean what he seemed to say and was not therefore an
aesthete. Ruth Child's book makes him out to be, except for some
early essays, really very wholesome and not "impressionist" in a
bad sense.[10] This of course can plausibly be done because Pater,
in the manner of English critics, *is* thoroughly inconsistent.
(They are like Dr. Johnson's Polly Carmichael: wiggle-waggle
and cannot be got to be categorical.) This being the case, I think
the most valuable single study of Pater is Helen Young's, which,
placing him in the context of contemporary thought, indicates
the shifts in meaning of his crucial words.[11] (No one has done
precisely this for Arnold.) Perhaps it is because Pater's thought is
various and hard to untangle that Brooks and Wimsatt in their
generally valuable and much needed history of criticism pass
him over with a mere mention and take as their pattern of
aesthetic doctrine Oscar Wilde. This, though a fashionable pro-

cedure, is to falsify the history of criticism, for as an influence Pater was of tremendous importance. (It is like using Catulle Mendès instead of Baudelaire to illustrate Symbolism.) Yeats writes in *The Trembling of the Veil,* "we looked consciously to Pater for our philosophy." [12] And Saintsbury in 1906 still believes, as he has for thirty years, that *Studies in the History of the Renaissance* "was, is, and is likely to remain one of the most noteworthy *points de repère* in the English literature of the late nineteenth century." "It seems also," he says, "that this book and some (not quite all) of those that followed, occupied and defined a critical standpoint which had been only occasionally reached, and never very definitely or consciously held, before." [13]

It is Pater who defines the aesthetic critic and impressionist criticism. It is a misreading of Pater that leads to the popular misconception of what happened to the artists of the nineties. Any reappraisal of the nineties must dwell at some length on this puzzling Oxford don.

Before coming to these important matters I should like to mention certain minor ways in which Pater forecasts our age. By his brooding attraction to sickness and death he reminds us of Thomas Mann. His significant moments of experience—moments which become ends in themselves—remind us of the illuminating and transcendent moments of Proust, Eliot, and Virginia Woolf. And in his sense of the essential and desolating loneliness of the human being he anticipates much of modern fiction. His *Imaginary Portraits* and *Marius,* interior portraits of curious personalities drawn against distinctive backgrounds in space and time, prove their author's sensibility to be of a sort not alien to the twentieth century. They should have their secure place in fiction.

I suspect that Pater's detractors would put his literary criticism there, too—if anywhere.

Now what is Pater's critical method? He defines his terms in the Preface to *Studies in the History of the Renaissance*. "To define beauty, not in the most abstract, but in the most concrete terms possible, to find, not a *universal formula* for it, but the formula which expresses most adequately this or that *special manifestation* of it, is the aim of the true student of aesthetics." Pater *says* "the true student of aesthetics," but I suspect that he is thinking rather of the practicing critic. For, as he goes on, we find that the aesthetic critic's business is to find in the object under discussion "the *virtue*" by which it operates aesthetically— that is, produces pleasure. Here is orthodox romantic doctrine (Coleridge had dared to use the word *pleasure* for the object of literature—however the word might dismay Victorians). But this orthodox theory is here more closely applied to the critic's function than is customary. Beauty being not general but singular, the special *quality* which distinguishes a work of art must be *felt* by the individual experiencing it, and this feeling will be a *unique impression* of pleasure. These things being true, the ideal critic will be one whose temperament inclines him to be deeply moved by beautiful objects—one is reminded of Wordsworth's poet: a man of "more than usual organic sensibility"—but of *different* kinds, for the characteristic beauties of all ages are of equal value. I have italicized the familiar key words of romanticism. The word which assumes spectacular importance from here on is *impression*. (I think a rather good case might be made out for impressionism as the general label of the new arts and of criticism from the 1870s on.) How, precisely, does the aesthetic critic go to work? His function is "to distinguish, analyse, and separate from its adjuncts, the virtue by which a picture . . . produces this special impression of beauty or pleasure, to indicate what the source of that impression is, and under what conditions it is experienced. His end is reached when he has disengaged that virtue, and noted it, as a chemist notes some natural element, for himself and others. . . ."[14] The critic then will not be content with having the *impression* of a characteristic pleasure; he will distinguish and analyze the elements in the work which produce that impression. This is the program of Baudelaire, who has been called the greatest of nineteenth century critics: "Je résolus de m'informer du pourquoi et de transformer ma volupté en connaissance." As a sensitive individual, the critic experiences the work and then finds out how it has impressed him in just that way. To be sure, no provision is made here for judging or comparing, but on the part of the romantic critic this is commendable abstention, for unique individuals are finally incomparable. Arnold's critic was to ascertain the best, but the techniques of evaluation provided for him by Arnold were either extra-literary or hopelessly unwieldy (i.e., the touchstones for poetic merit).

The critic must, finally, somehow communicate his findings: he must note the virtue for himself and others. I suspect that it is especially in his execution of that step, conveying the aesthetic experience, that Pater incurs suspicion today. Let me remind you of the passage on *La Gioconda*. Yeats thought it worth including in the *Oxford Book of Modern Verse* as both poetry and a period piece. On neither ground would it rate high marks today. We have heard so often that it puts one work in place of another that we have long ago ceased, I suspect, to try to see any correspondence between painting and words. But what if Pater's (and Swinburne's?) "vision" has a significant relation to Leonardo's? Fernandez in *Messages* has a suggestive description of Pater's procedure: "With criticism-metaphors, with cycles of thought released by the strong spring of impression, he envelopes the latter with concentric intellectual lines, he elucidates it, erects and orders it on the plane of consciousness." [15] Metaphor as a critical device.[16] For how *is* one to convey the quality of a work of art? (Remember that the *good* work is one in which form and content are *fused,* for all arts approach the condition of music.) The romantic critic has had his Image (or impression) of the work and this he *evokes* by means of his own creation. It is the procedure of symbolist poetry as Symons describes it: "To evoke by some elaborate instantaneous magic of language without the formality of an after all impossible description; to be, in fact, rather than to express. . . ." [17] Pater's criticism of a work might then be called the objective correlative of the original. Of course this elevates the critic to the status of creator—but where is the harm? Can the critic in fact be *un*creative?

But then the question arises: why not simply experience the work for ourselves, why the intermediary vision? And this leads us to consider the critic's audience. Romantic criticism is not addressed to the artist. Since Pater published in the great established reviews, the *Fortnightly,* the *Contemporary,* he presumably addressed a public, as it were, moderately literate, acquainted with the works discussed (at least in the case of the Renaissance studies) but less well acquainted than the critic, willing to have more light on the unfamiliar, a public which might be induced by some such epiphany as a Pater Image to try his own reading or re-reading, viewing or re-viewing.

Does modern textual criticism—that of the New Critics, for

example—do more or as much? The abundance of existing textual commentaries on the poems of Yeats and Eliot does not invariably serve the purpose of illuminating the texts of these difficult poets. Graduate students, even, are sometimes led to lose the poem in a thicket of conflicting interpretations (of parts, too, rather than wholes) and to allow themselves to be persuaded that what could provoke such diversity of comment must remain impenetrable. What would be the common reader's response to these inscrutable performances on the critical instrument daunts the imagination. But of course the common reader is still less likely to read Empson on Eliot than Eliot. Apparently Pater *was* read by the subscribers to the *Contemporary* and the *Fortnightly*. Today the great reviews are no more, for the common reader of our day is not the man he used to be. And indeed the New Critic addresses not the common man but the intellectual or the academic. Who is in the ivory tower now?

Criticism has indeed ramified into schools so diverse in their interests that a survey of twentieth-century criticism proposes as the ideal of the future criticism by committee. (The word used is *symposium,* but that seems unnecessarily grandiose.) I can think of one further step. It has been taken in the matters of correcting examinations, predicting weather, and translating books. Why not a machine to process the data and come up with the summation (*conclusion* or *evaluation* would again be too grandiose)? As weighed against the criticism that is art-seen-through-a-temperament, which seems to hold more promise?

Modern critics, diverse as they are, may, however, be divided into two main groups: those who regard literature as literature and those who regard it as something else, for example, an expression of Freudian impulses, an argument for one or another interpretation of history or society, a revelation of man's tribal instincts. The second group, I suspect, does not really want to tell us about literature at all. They are writing footnotes to anthropology, sociology, economics, psychology. Just here is where the lesson of the ivory tower comes in. Art may of course be used to document the human situation. But it is a document because it is an autonomous activity of mankind (possibly his distinctive one). Art is *for* art as pure science is for science. It is the peculiar virtue of the aesthetic critic to treat it thus. Pater showed the way and the New Critic follows his illumination (though often, it appears, ignorant of its source). Here, then, is one illustration of the ivory tower as lighthouse.

About Pater too little has recently been said; about Oscar Wilde so much is written that he may be said to be the only figure of the nineties who today enjoys a popular survival. I find this a case of unnatural selection, and I am at a loss to account for it. His books are given new editions from year to year; the Viking Portable series has consecrated by excerpting him; scholars explore facts of his life and art for doctoral and other purposes. His comedies—often revived—succeed like the similar veneered trivialities of Noel Coward. The style of the fairy stories and *Dorian Gray* is ornate and sentimental—the style of the nineties at its worst—and one would suppose it unlikely to appeal to an age nourished, if that is the word, on Hemingway and Steinbeck and Dos Passos. But perhaps he affords the complex experience of pleasure in his sophisticated sentimentality, mixed with condescension; for is he not a period piece of a "ridiculous" period that he helped to make ridiculous?

Possibly The Decadence would have seemed less decadent had Wilde not furnished it with an object lesson. It was too perfectly pat that the very model of the Aesthetic should have justified the settled convictions of Mrs. Grundy and come to grief, paid his debt to society, written the "Ballad of Reading Gaol" and disappeared. Wilde tried so hard to incarnate the aesthetic movement that I suppose even responsible writers must be pardoned if they conclude that he did. And his *Intentions* is such a handy compendium of the basic thought of other men, his masters—for he was always the disciple—that historians of literature may be tempted to prefer it as a document to its more complex sources.

What the parable of Wilde illustrates of course is not at all the doctrine of art for art's sake [18] (that is the part of Flaubert, the ascetic of letters), but the quite separate and indeed opposite one of *life as art.* It is only by accident of historical juxtaposition that these two contrary notions come to be confused. For *life* as a fine art, Pater provided the text in the Conclusion to the *Renaissance.* This set piece is so notorious that I suspect no one reads it, and thus its extraordinary relevance to modern life and art has escaped notice. Like so much of Pater's writing, it expresses the impact of science on modern man, and in its preoccupation with the fleeting nature of experience, the isolation of human beings, the relation of consciousness to the objects of consciousness, it outlines the program of the modern psychological novel. The central core is the problem of human personality, shifting, too, in the physical world of flux. All being transient and relative, including man, how is man to live? "What we have to do is to be for ever curiously testing new opinions and courting new impressions, never acquiescing in a facile orthodoxy of

Comte, or of Hegel or of our own." In part this essay reads like a prospectus for a progressive college: beware of sacrificing our experience for some interest into which we cannot enter or some abstract theory we have not identified ourselves with or what is only conventional. In part it is *Faust* brought up to date: "Not the fruit of experience, but experience itself is the end." In this new version, however, it is *art* that will give the highest quality to your moments as they pass. And here, Yeats tells us, is the directive that led the tragic generation to walk upon a tight-rope[19] and Wilde in particular to go about proclaiming the gospel of beauty but exhibiting not a trace of concern for art as the *artist* must concern himself with art. Yeats saw clearly that there were two ways:

> The intellect of man is forced to choose
> Perfection of the life, or of the work,
> And if it take the second must refuse
> A heavenly mansion, raging in the dark.
>
> ("The Choice")

Wilde was no watcher in the ivory tower. His sphere, like that of the "Great Victorians," was *action;* and, as Yeats has noted, "his plays and dialogues have what merit they possess from being now an imitation, now a record, of his talk."[20]

It has been claimed for Wilde that he had a share in opening England to the new art of France (with which he was indeed familiar), but his role was inconsiderable as compared with that of Swinburne, Moore, and Symons. He did, of course, use the names and phrases of Gautier and Flaubert, as he used the ideas of these and of his English predecessors and contemporaries.

Reading *Intentions* one finds here a bit of Arnold, here a patch of Pater or William Morris, and, in this unlikely company, even Carlyle. On the whole he must have done the aesthetic cause more harm than good, for, as in Victorian England one so outrageously unconventional could not be taken seriously, the ridicule and then the odium he incurred came to adhere also to the ideas he stood or was supposed to stand for.[21]

As in Pater (and some of them *from* Pater) there are in Wilde's witty dialogue "The Critic as Artist" (*Intentions*) ideas that anticipate twentieth-century art and criticism. These occur rather as maxims than as part of a coherent theory, so, yielding on my own part to the temptation to use the popularizer, I shall note a few of them *seriatim*. Here are some of Wilde's ideas which are implied or explicit in most modern criticism. The critic is not confined to discovering the artist's *intention,* for the meaning of a work is as much in the mind of the one who reads as of the artist. The critic prefers to simple modes of art those whose imaginative beauty makes "all interpretations true and none final." (The latter modes are today a boon to the analogy-finder and myth-man, and the next statement will show one of the dangers of their critical procedures.) The critic as interpreter passes "from his sympathetic impression of the work as a whole to analysis or exposition"—but this analysis may deepen the mystery, showing as it does the difficulty of appreciating art. The critic is always showing the work of art in a new relation to our age. (This one points to Eliot and Brooks on the romantics.) The creator is always behind the times; it is the critic who leads the way. (There is precisely the point I am trying to make about the nineties, and here is another which might be seriously considered in the twentieth-century context.) The future belongs to the critics, for though much remains to be done by the artist in the realm of introspection, "the *habit* of introspection may prove fatal to [the] creative faculty." Yeats, the great modern creator, has observed:

> We have lit upon the gentle, sensitive mind
> And lost the old nonchalance of the hand;
> Whether we have chosen chisel, pen or brush
> We are but critics or but half create.
>
> ("Ego Dominus Tuus")

On art in general here are a few of the observations from "The Critic as Artist" or "The Decay of Lying" (*Intentions*). Language, which raises man above the animals, is the *parent* of thought. Form suggests content and is all important. Imagination is concentrated race experience. Art is necessary because life is deficient in form: one cannot repeat the same emotion. (Of this Proust provides an illustration: his fictional life is constructed as an art object in which moments *can* be relived.) Finally—a crucial idea of the aesthetic school in France—the true imaginative work must be prepared for by the deliberate rejection of ordinary imitation and of nature as an ideal of beauty. Art is our gallant protest against nature. This is the Baudelaire-dandy trend of the times and, of all Wilde's pronouncements, the one, I should imagine, that fell with most devastating effect on Victorian ears. In France such a statement would seem unexceptionable, but to the Englishman nature is only a shade less sacred than Britannia. From the Renaissance onward a conventional opposition was made by English writers between French artists, inferior because their allegiance was to *art,* and English, who virtuously imitated nature. (One has only to compare the gardens of the Tuileries and Regent's Park to observe that the national preferences still hold good.) The aesthetic movement could not fail to arouse philistine ire, for to the suspicion incurred by any group of writers flaunting worship of art was added the distaste that since the Renaissance has marked for the British middle class any importation from France. It was nineteenth-century France that originated the new modes in literature and art of our century. And it was through English critics from the 1860s on that England reentered the stream of Continental literature, French modes were made available to creative writers, and a British audience gradually prepared for these novelties. It was not an easy conquest, for British romantics and Victorians had ignored or detested or at best condescended to all the French literature and painting of which they had been made aware. It required the concentrated effort of many—of whom Wilde was only one and, as I have suggested, too notorious to inspire confidence in his own age and too derivative to deserve very well of ours.

Two other tenders of the lighthouse lamp deserve more of our notice than they have so far enjoyed. Both disciples of Pater, they used, to a greater extent than he, the lessons learned of French artists and critics to enrich and illustrate their critical theory and method. The first, George Moore, is a far better exponent than Oscar Wilde of art for art's sake; the second, Arthur Symons, a better impressionist critic.

It was in France, where he spent seven formative years, that Moore learned how art should not serve any master, or the artist any public, but where he learned, too, that the artist must devote himself unremittingly to his craft. These lessons he never forgot, and he is the closest parallel among English artists to Flaubert, as concerned as he with the word and the sentence, like him experimental, differing, of course, in concept of style and in a more exuberant temperament so that he served the exacting muse more gaily.

Marius and *Mademoiselle de Maupin* were at first his golden books, but his first novels were patterned after the realistic Flaubert and Huysmans and the naturalistic Goncourts and Zola, and thus he was led into the battle of the circulating libraries. As the poet Swinburne had been drawn into pamphleteering in defense of the artist's freedom in the 1870s, so Moore defended his most naturalistic novel (*A Mummer's Wife*) with a pamphlet, *Literature at Nurse, or Circulating Morals* (1885), aimed at the moralistic censorship of Mudie's. The result, Brown says in his book on Moore, was that "the British public moved slightly toward toleration for writers for the first time in half a century." [22] How far the public and the circulating libraries had to go before the English novelist had won the freedom he now enjoys may be estimated if one recalls the vicissitudes of Hardy's novels and even of *Richard Feverel*. But that the artist *does* now enjoy this freedom he owes in large part to the critical effort of the post-Victorian writers who fought under the banner of Gautier. Art need not serve the moral conventions of any segment of society, he had said. For art, the *perfection of form* is virtue. Literature need not be written so as to preserve the innocence of the *jeune fille*. Here is a notable debt of our age to the aesthetic critic—and in part to George Moore.

Moore should have his place in the Pantheon—there are some

signs that he may eventually achieve it—not only for his novels but even more for his peculiarly personal genre, the conversational, reminiscent essay that ranges here and there as memory dictates. In *Impressions and Opinions, Avowals,* and *Conversations in Ebury Street* we find his unsystematic criticism which pretends to be no more than a reflection of his temperament but is always entertaining and often perceptive. Through these essays (and others), examples of impressionist criticism, he made known in England (in many cases for the first time) the impressionist painters and French writers who were to change the course of English painting, poetry, and fiction.

In the last analysis, should not criticism be readable? Moore's is, and rereadable too. And if it does not compel assent it may serve the useful purpose of sending the reader to the books. Moreover, it is craftsman's criticism, always aware of the problems of the writer.

Arthur Symons enjoys one distinction denied to other critics of the nineties. The two great poets of our time have publicly expressed their debt to his *Symbolist Movement in Literature.* What this book did was to define and describe the new poetry of France and thus to make available in England the conception of poetry which is, I suppose, still the prevailing one in both France and England. Like Moore, Symons was more than critic. Indeed it is as poet that he would wish to be remembered. His poetry deserves more recognition than it has had: *historically,* for it illustrates the current notion of impressionist verse and its relation to the symbol; *aesthetically,* for it is various and sometimes good. His verse translations, too, are by no means negligible. And any study of Symons as critic must take account of Symons the poet, for as the criticism he practiced was impressionist, his temperament as poet helps to explain the inclusions, omissions, excellences.

It is as critic, I think, that he is most important, and perhaps as critic of French literature. Quantitatively his work as intermediary was voluminous, comprehending not only essays on but translations and editions of writers from Villon on. Unlike Arnold, he wrote most often on the important writers and in many cases he was the first to mention a particular French writer in England. Since he knew French and his contemporaries in France, his criticism is almost always free from the usual English prejudice. And having a theoretical cast of mind he carried on in the nineties Pater's work of examining the aesthetic presuppositions of art—in his case especially the new art. He saw the importance in his time of the *transposition des arts*—the tendency to assimilate poetry to music or painting, painting and music to poetry. What this assimilation implies, related as it is to the crucial meanings of symbol and impression, has yet to be adequately studied, but a study would need to begin with the books Symons says he intended as a systematic investigation of the problem: after *The Symbolist Movement* (1899), *Plays, Acting and Music* (1903) and *Studies in Seven Arts* (1906). There is no doubt that the example of the visual arts, where the spectator readily forgets to demand a moral, helped the aesthetes in their struggle to establish autonomy in literature. Moore was always quoting Gautier: "I am a man for whom the visible world exists." Symons saw further than Moore though less far than Yeats into the complexities of the relation of visible to invisible worlds and this insight lends subtlety to his appreciation of the new art and, incidentally, of Blake.

As concerned as Pater with style, his own was more flexible

than Pater's, more neutral, perhaps, and so may be less disconcerting to the twentieth-century reader.

There are many other critics who ought to figure here: Saintsbury surely, who preached and practiced aesthetic criticism and whose critical output was stupendous; Henry James for his "Art of Fiction" (1888) and his perplexed relation to the French novelists; Lionel Johnson for his study of Hardy (1894). Whistler's *Ten O'Clock* began the decade (1890), and the "incomparable Max" published his "complete" works in 1896. The high standard of journalism in the era is conspicuous (and this topic is relatively unexplored). Little magazines like the *Savoy* and the *Dome* attracted distinguished writers and illustrators. Oxford dons and Edinburgh professors wrote respectable and remunerative articles for the great monthlies and quarterlies—which (except occasionally in name) have vanished from the democratic scene. Though I may have managed to convey an impression only of the strangeness of nineties' criticism, the period was both strange and rich. Scholarship of a "modern" kind flourished on very nearly a modern scale. Many series of reprints from the classics, English and foreign, were undertaken. In these ten years were published Gosse's *History of English Literature* (1897), Saintsbury's *Essays on French Novelists* (1891) and *Short History of French Literature* (1897), Dowden's *History of French Literature* (1897) and *Literary Criticism in France* (1900). Wagner was defended (Shaw's *The Perfect Wagnerite,* 1898). Translation abounded, from French, German, and Russian—and everyone knows about Ibsen in the nineties (see Shaw's *Quintessence of Ibsenism,* 1891). Havelock Ellis wrote enthusiastically on Zola, Casanova, Huysmans, Nietzsche (*Affirmations,* 1898).

It was the 1890s, precisely insofar as they were not Victorian, that began the literature of our age. If we find among the new men a plenitude of minor figures, let us remind ourselves that the eighteenth-century romantics were not for the most part major figures either. The eighteenth century had its Blake, and in the Rhymers' Club took shape the art of William Butler Yeats, one cygnet among the ducklings. He has done rather better by the associates of his early days—those poets unhonored and unsung —than have professional scholars.[23] Indeed no professional scholar thus far has provided the reassessment which nineteenth-century literature deserves. When Stanley Edgar Hyman (in *The Armed Vision*) can find modern criticism emerging only in 1923 with Richards's *Principles of Literary Criticism,* we must convict ourselves of taking our premises as shoppers take a tram. For the criticism of the twentieth century has its roots in the aesthetic movement, which evolved the related theories of impressionist criticism and the autonomy of art. The second gave the artist the freedom to create and the critic a related point of view. The first gave the critic the grounds for handling literature (which is still romantic) in a manner consistent with romantic doctrine. In the world of horizontal man, the ivory tower of the aesthetic artist-critic has served as lighthouse for the art and criticism of our time. It has shown the way.

⅀⅄

The Nineties: Beginning, End, or Transition?

HELMUT E. GERBER

Discussions of the nineties sometimes resemble the hieroglyphics in the book by Nostrodamus' hand. Fortunately, it requires no Faust to recognize the signs pointing at three approaches to this decade: the first is represented by "young-manism," "dash for life," beginning; the second by *fin de siècle,* senility, death, ending; and the third by experimentation, transition.

Under these three heads, beginning, end, and transition, I shall examine two aspects of the web of commentary that literary historians have woven around the nineties: the question of the time span and the question of characteristics. Within this framework I hope to suggest a context for the nineties, something of the content, and, by way of conclusion, a little of the challenge that is still to be met.

I

In view of the fact that I am discussing the 1890s, to raise the question "from when to when?" at all may seem unnecessary. But the term nineties, like the term *fin de siècle,* has through usage become prickly with meanings. It does not mean 1890 to 1900, or, rather, it includes this among its meanings, as the phrase "Victorian period" includes 1837 to 1901 among its meanings. I must raise the question of the time span because the intricate discussions of the genesis of the nineties vary in establishing the origin of the period from the Council of Trent to the year 1895.

Literary historians give various accounts of how and when the nineties began. First, there is the account of cataclysmic beginnings. According to Frances Winwar, for example,

> The old century was dying, but in the man-made concept of time, that death betokened a beginning. Heavy with life the chrysalis was about to burst with the century born of the old, yet, for the hopes of mankind, a brighter and more wonderful harbinger of futurity.[1]

The nineties, then, burst upon the world as the start of a new age. When we turn to Bernard Muddiman's account, we suspect that Miss Winwar's chrysalis may have contained Aubrey Beardsley, for "The day Beardsley left his stool and ledger in a London insurance office and betook himself seriously to the illustration of the strange comic world of Congreve, a new manifestation of English art blossomed." [2] This was apparently in August of 1892, although, as Mr. Muddiman later tells us, Beardsley's "seedtime" conveniently came between 1889 and 1891. Soon the *"enfant terrible"* burst out of the chrysalis, a full-fledged moth "burning, burning," and at the age of twenty-one illustrated the *Morte d'Arthur* for Dent. Muddiman, like Miss Winwar, also modifies his view in several places, but the emphasis is on the sudden arrival of Beardsley as herald of the Beardsley period. Edmund Gosse, writing in 1897, arrives at much the same view of beginnings by way of a familiar system of astrology. "We may anticipate," he says, "that future historians may make that date [Tennyson's death] the starting point for a new era. . . . Up to 1892, certainly, we can affirm the maintenance, without radical change of any kind, of the original romantic system. . . ."[3] For Blaikie Murdoch, too, this "war-like" period began "almost exactly in 1890, while it ended almost exactly at the beginning of the twentieth century,"[4] for Symons's *Days and Nights* "sounded a revolutionary note" in 1889 and the young men died young at the turn of the century.

The second account of beginnings is akin to Darwin's theory of evolutionary descent. Darwin's bulldog in this instance is Osbert Burdett. "The point of view," he writes in *The Beardsley Period* (1925), "was called *fin de siècle* . . . but the cycle that it seemed to close was longer than a hundred years." Burdett begins with "the disruption of the medieval mould," takes the reader through the "ensuing mood . . . of gathering disillusion . . . until at the end of three hundred years—for the year 1859 [when the prophetic Darwin apparently provided the great revelation] is the second date we shall notice—the cycle traversed seemed complete, and a new hypothesis gave an unexpected sanction to the modern attitude. Of this," Burdett continues, "the nineties may, I think, be regarded as the culmination, and the object of the following excursion is to see the decade in the stream of change." In this account, it seems to me, the *fin de siècle* trails behind it a rather unwieldy tail, with Copernicus, Bruno, Galileo, Shakespeare, Dr. Johnson, Wordsworth, Emily Brontë, and Darwin encumbered in its coils. "The course traversed by the modern mind," we are told, "was complete, and the alpha and omega of its progress are the Tridentine Council and *The Origin of Species*." [5]

A third account of the when and how of the nineties might be labeled psychological or psychiatric. In its Thanatopsis emphasis, as in Max Nordau's *Degeneration* [despite prefatory modifications], or, more moderately, in Murdoch's *The Renaissance of the Nineties* (1911), or in Malcolm Elwin's *Old Gods Falling* (1939), it is Freudian. In its emphasis on the *libido* as the will to live, as in Holbrook Jackson's "dash for life," or J. Lewis May's notion of a centrifugal force converging on the fountain of youth provided by Lane and Matthews in Vigo Street, it is Jungian.[6] The basic observation seems to be that at the ends of centuries, though not necessarily in the last decade only, human beings, but artists in particular, are infected by a sense of death, decay, agony, old gods falling, cultural decline, on the one hand, or by a sense of regeneration, at least a newness of some kind, on the other.

Sometimes, however, complexity is compounded when the same phenomenon is understood to represent both life and death. Thus, decadence is often viewed as a bell tolling to the death agony of the last Romantics or the last Victorians and at the same time ringing in the New Morality, the New Realism, the New Journalism, the New Woman, and perhaps even, as in a way Ruth Temple has suggested the aesthetic critics do, heralding the New Criticism. In fact, almost all the analysts intent on proving the patient healthy and sane observe that genuine decadence in the nineties *is* a renaissance. There is a little hint of this idea of health in sickness in Manlio Miserochi's comment that the individualistic principles of Oscar Wilde are the forces for a healthier future society.[7] Something of the kind also seems true of some views of symbolism, as in Paul Valéry's remark that the symbolist movement on the one hand negated ethical and traditional values and on the other asserted "absolute adventure in the realm of artistic creation."[8] So, also, Holbrook Jackson writes that "the decadence reveals qualities which, even if nothing more than 'the soul of goodness in things evil,' are at times surprisingly excellent."[9] Viewed in this way, the period becomes phoenix-like.

The historian of ideas seems to hold that the point of view of the nineties is one which has, with various modifications, evolved at various times in man's cultural history. He tends to find a dominant leitmotif (symbolism, decadence, aestheticism, naturalism) and then to equate it with the whole period. Others, placing less emphasis on historical echoings but not excluding them entirely, stress an hour and a man. Thus, the hour is the death of Tennyson or the appearance of *Days and Nights;* the man is Oscar Wilde or Aubrey Beardsley or, for that matter, John Lane. In fact, a comment of Richard Le Gallienne seems to imply that the chief unifying characteristic of the nineties is Bodleyheadism. Those who place the emphasis on a mood resulting from some inherent association with the ends and beginnings of centuries tend to melodramatize the twilight of the gods by oversimplifying or distorting the often contradictory characteristics of the period, and by overlooking the fact that calendars do not control men. A similar fallacy is to equate the eccentricities of a small group with the "period-mind."

My own position is not so high-flown.[10] I recognize a distinct period between about 1880 and about 1920, or, more flexibly, between 1870 and 1930. I do not regard the nineties as significantly a genesis of anything, and the decade seems to me not to be significantly the end of anything. For me this decade is not an independent, more or less self-sufficient period, even if it is limited to the works of a handful of young men who died relatively young. It is a colorful, fervent, sometimes clamorous, often comic and just as often tragic decade in the heart of a cultural period which can best be denoted with the words "interim," "experimentation," "turning point," or "transition."

The word "transition" is, in fact, used and the idea of a turning point suggested in a number of published works to characterize the period I am describing. For example, Frederic Harrison writes in 1893, "We live . . . in an age of transition; we are trying new lines of activity; and we are making some crucial experiments"; [11] A. J. Farmer, addressing himself to the aesthetic and decadent movements in England, holds that *"la période qui va de 1880 à 1900 environ marque un tournant dans l'évolution intellectuelle et morale de l'Europe";* [12] and many other writers, in book and chapter titles as in the central theses of their works, describe the period in the same way.[13]

What was happening in the nineties had been going on since the 1870s. There certainly was no single shot heard around the world that can fairly be blamed or praised as the impulse that set the activities of the nineties—or of the period from 1870 to 1930—in motion. It was not simply Mundella's compulsory education bill of 1870 as Edward Scouller has it, nor the Elementary Education Act of 1870 as Walter Murdoch and A. J. Philip have it, nor was it Zola's naturalism or Huysmans's "spiritualistic naturalism" as Frierson has it.[14] Rather this period evolved slowly during the seventies and eighties out of a multitude of events and influences. The last twenty to thirty years of the nineteenth century witnessed the rise, almost concurrently, of half a dozen literary movements as well as many momentous political, economic, and moral shifts of emphasis. These currents interacted upon each other in a way that almost defies our efforts to oversimplify the process by applying an adamantine nomenclature to all the changes we can catch in flight.

What was happening in the nineties, as Walter E. Houghton has also suggested,[15] continued to happen well into the 1920s: generally, vigorous experimentation, journeys out in all directions; more specifically, further fictional probing into the darker corners of the conscious and subconscious mind; further experiments in the fusing of fiction with musical forms and with techniques borrowed from painting; and further investigations into the possibility of combining the recording of literal fact and evocative symbol. While the essential spirit remained the same, the nomenclature changed almost from year to year. The hue and cry becomes Dadaism and surrealism instead of decadence and symbolism; cubism and futurism instead of impressionism; psychological realism instead of naturalism; relativism instead of positivism; Marxism and Communism instead of Fabianism. If there has been a pause such as G. K. Chesterton and Elizabeth Bowen have alluded to,[16] then it was after Joyce's *Ulysses* appeared, after Lawrence's major novels were published, after Virginia Woolf's *To the Lighthouse* and *Mrs. Dalloway* came out, and after Dorothy Richardson's *Pointed Roofs* found its way into the hands of those who read novelists' novels. The period, not so much of exhaustion, but of stocktaking, came in the late 1920s and early 1930s.

The decade of the nineties is for me a clearing house of ideas and techniques. It is, as Havelock Ellis says in a more general application, "the shifting point at which past and future meet, and we can have no quarrel with either." "Transition," the term I have been insisting upon, implies some continuity between the two periods on either side. This is perhaps another way of saying that we ought to distinguish between a period which is a whole loaf and a decade which is a slice. Nor ought we to confuse a whole pollywog with merely the tail of the one that went before.

II

Decadence, aestheticism, naturalism, impressionism, symbolism, neo-romanticism, late Victorianism, modernism, and a host of other isms—these are some of the movements, whenever they began, that commentators recognize in the nineties. What general label really fits a period in which there are so many major movements and characteristics, all apparently overlapping if not exactly coincident? The late H. M. Tomlinson calls his book on his youth at the end of the Victorian era *A Mingled Yarn;* "An intricate tapestry" some of us might prefer to call the nineties and their environs. It is, I think, exactly this interweaving of threads that characterizes the period and distinguishes it from other periods. It is the *particular* combination of many major forces, not merely complexity as such, that distinguishes the period.

Not only has the search for a simple label given a distorted view of the nineties but also the tendency to follow up an un-considered antagonism to the literature of the time with a thoroughly condemnatory tag.[17] The tendency in books pub-lished between 1893 and about 1925 was to label all the new movements as in some way decadent, often with the same im-plication of moral judgment that was applied to the decadent movement itself, and sometimes with the same tone of aggressive defensiveness used by the supporters of the decadence. In any event, in the popular mind, the word "decadence" had been applied to French writers whose works were associated with a morbid imagination, a fondness for corpses, diseases, physical, mental, and moral degeneracy of all kinds. But in England the term quite early began to sweep into the same heap much other literary subject matter, especially if it could be associated with French sources.

Thus, by 1893 Nordau could throw together three forms of degeneracy, each with its related sub-elements: (1) mysticism (Pre-Raphaelites, symbolism, Tolstoyism, the Richard Wagner cult); (2) ego-mania (Parnassians and diabolists, decadents and aesthetes, Ibsenism, Nietzscheans); and (3) realism (Zola and his school, the "Young German" plagiarists). Under the single rubric "degeneracy," Nordau too facilely encompasses all the leitmotifs that one can discover between about 1870 and 1893. The only writers to survive this "black death of degeneration and hysteria" will be those capable of precise observation, those less given to wild imagining. In fact, he hints that imaginative litera-ture may play a smaller role in the twentieth century than it had. While Nordau mistakenly insists that most of these movements are "unfit" and would thus, by means of a kind of cultural jungle law, become extinct, and that "emancipation from traditional discipline" is a major evil, he does correctly recognize the interrelationship of these various movements.

The many facets of decadence are also illustrated by Arthur Symons's several discussions of Verlaine's work. Symons, who was to come to the defense of most of the modern movements in the arts, in 1891 had sufficient distrust of symbolism and decadence to separate Verlaine from these labels, but in 1892 he took a milder tone toward the two movements, and in his 1893 "The Decadent Movement in Literature," he includes Verlaine.[18] The aesthetic movement, which Walter Hamilton had praised in *The Aesthetic Movement in England* (1882), had apparently so conditioned the decadent and naturalist movements, which Nordau damned, that in Symons's criticism, as Clarence Decker suggests, "Aestheticism and Naturalism are united in Symbolism," [19] a remark similar to the point Edmund Wilson made in a broader sense, that "the literary history of our time is to a great extent that of the development of symbolism and its fusion or conflict with naturalism." [20] Walter Hamilton, in any event, as early as 1882 had recognized the fusion of various experiments. Like Nordau, he had noted the connection of Wagner with the aesthetic movement, the general aim of the movement to relate the several arts, the inseparability of aestheticism and realism, the relationship of the movement to the earlier romanticism, and the essential quality of intensity which was later to be discovered in decadence. Hamilton only objects to the superficial aestheticism of "the school of artistic slang and stained-glass attitudes," but, unlike Nordau, he does not regard the genuine aestheticism as degenerate.

We observe this same interrelationship of movements in George Moore, who while still under the naturalist influence was also introducing the French symbolists to the English reading public, although as Bruce Morrissette observes, with a superficial understanding.[21] Robert J. Barnes, in his University of Texas dissertation, "George Moore and the Arts," has more sympathetically suggested that "Moore's use of the fine arts (particularly music and painting) in his prose fiction" shows him to be "a precursor of the moderns in his use of theme and symbol, as well as technique." So, also, in Oscar Wilde's work when taken together, we receive a total impression not of a decadent or an aesthete, but of a many-faceted artist discovering new relationships. His *Dorian Gray,* for example, can, I think, be viewed as an attempted synthesis of the several movements in the arts up to its writing. Wilde's criticism and especially his sympathetic appreciation of Balzac's realism also suggest a more balanced artistic theory than Wilde is generally credited with. Richard Le Gallienne has, in fact, said that Wilde is the "astonishing, impudent microcosm" who emerged out of the 1890 chaos, for Wilde was "the synthesis of all these phenomena of change."[22] Even Bernard Shaw, in Margaret Schlauch's article "Symbolic Figures and the Symbolic Technique of George Bernard Shaw,"[23] has been shown to fuse the various currents of the time, flowing through Ibsen, Wagner, the Fabians, and Sir James Fraser's work.

In two articles first published in *Forum* in 1893, Frederic Harrison also labels the period decadent, but he too has difficulty in making the term apply simply and narrowly to an age of fusing literary experiments.[24] Writing from the point of view of the positivist synthesis but without apparently realizing that synthesis is what was going on during the period, Harrison inveighs against the specialism of the age which he says is "most antipathetic to Art." Many paintings, he writes, were mere transcripts "from hospitals, police cells, and dens of infamy. . . . But the aim of these modern 'artists' is not art—but disgust," a comment as often applied to naturalism as to decadence. "The essential claim of 'modernity,' " he goes on, "is to assert the absolute independence of Art, and to defy any sort of condition of limit, whether of tradition, philosophy, morality, or even good sense." At the same time he recognizes in "many of these efforts after a new type . . . some of the most hopeful signs of our time. Especially is that true of those poetic efforts to combine fact, beauty, pathos, and reality in the aspect of common things and lowly lives. . . ."

Under the heading of romanticism, J. M. Kennedy, in *English Literature, 1880–1905* (1907),[25] discusses many of the same ideas that others treat under decadence, aestheticism, or naturalism. Classical restraint, he insists, has been overthrown by a romantic mood. "Melancholy is the keynote of the last generation of English literature," and the key phrases are "artistic impotence," "artistic philistinism," "weakness of will." The gloom descended when, prior to 1880, religion ceased to be the mainstay of creative artists and when Hellenism became misunderstood. However, although unable to discover a Goethe capable of bringing the romantic and Hellenic elements into balance, Kennedy does find five writers (Pater, Wilde, Davidson, Symons, and Gissing) who were aware of classicism and showed they were trying to achieve, as he says, a "higher aim than that which the average romanticist has in view." Of these five writers, Davidson comes closest to the classical ideal. In fact, I might note that Davidson's own comment on his work, that the old and new are ever "weltering upon the borders of my world," may be suggestive of the balance Kennedy has in mind. It might also be well to recall at this point that, whatever the shortcomings of his book, William Gaunt, in *Victorian Olympus* (1952), has interestingly discussed the classical revival in painting at the end of the nineteenth century, and that Lewis Mumford, in his review of A. J. Farmer's book on the aesthetic and decadent movements, has suggested the importance of studying the influence of the Greek Anthology and the relationship of Latin and Greek erotic poetry to the literature of the last decades of the nineteenth century.[26]

In his slender but still interesting *The Renaissance of the Nineties* (1911),[27] W. G. Blaikie Murdoch also discusses the nineties under the rubric "Little Romanticism." After a period of artistic sterility or literary anemia, he maintains, came the 1880s, "a time of transition, a period of simmering for revolt rather than actual outbreak," and then the nineties, an age of small giants, witnessed a "small repetition of the Renaissance of Wonder in the time of Blake." The contrast between the nineties and the sixties, between the art of nerves and the art of muscle, is the core of Murdoch's discussion. The art of the nineties deals with the actual circumstances of the artists' lives, it is concerned with "the statement of the present"; life is the watchword, the emphasis is on the city, on Fleet Street and London suburbs, rather than on exotic ruins and mythological locales. Whereas the painters of the sixties dealt with Ophelias, knights-errant, and magic casements, the artists of the nineties depicted models dressing, music hall activity, a coster girl, and tea in a garden. In the treatment of character, Murdoch finds, the men of the nineties turn from an emphasis on deeds to an emphasis on thought, and they penetrate deeper into the inner lives of their people. This is much the same point made by Thomas Parkinson in his "Intimate and Impersonal: An Aspect of Modern Poetics," in which he finds the source for this introspection in "Pater's essay on style, with its stress on the individuality of the artist, seeing poetry as the expression of a unique soul with a unique view of the world." [28] Among other traits of the period, Murdoch lists greater freedom in selecting what is fit subject matter for art, opposition to the application of narrow moral strictures to art, the defense of truth to personal visions of life, where morbidity and unhealthiness had a place. Thus, under the tag "The Little Renaissance of Wonder," Murdoch combines elements of decadence, aestheticism, and naturalism to characterize the period.

In his chapter on "The Break-up of the Compromise," in *The Victorian Age in Literature* (1913), Chesterton, like Nordau but without the Viennese writer's vituperative manner, links the aesthetes and decadents, both under the leadership of Oscar Wilde, and attacks both movements. He prefers to use the words "exhaustion" and "queer" to describe the period which in a 1917 article he was also to call "decadent." [29] For Chesterton, as in part for Kennedy, the period witnessed the "coincident collapse of both religious and political idealism" which "produced a curious cold air of emptiness and real subconscious agnosticism." Chesterton does find a sound link with the live future in Wilde's *The Ballad of Reading Gaol,* the link with the socialist movement out of which came Wells and Shaw. In his 1917 article, he adds the pure note of Francis Thompson, although not a dominant one, to the signs of life in a period largely depicted by similes of death.

Bernard Muddiman limits himself strictly and narrowly to the so-called young men, Conder, Dowson, Crackanthorpe, Harland, and Symons, with Beardsley as the central figure. For him, too, the nineties is an "age of nerves" in the sense that there was "a keener sensitiveness to certain feelings in the art of this movement." According to Muddiman, "the majority of the work of the movement can be described as impressionism of the abnormal by a group of individualists," and the "predominant keynote will be found to be a keen sense of that strangeness of proportion which Bacon noted as characteristic of what he called beauty." This keynote in turn brought "a sense of freedom" and a desire "to emancipate our literature to the same extent as the literature of Latin countries." [30] This idea of a little renaissance, whether called romanticism or decadence or a movement of young men, is also at the heart of Burdett's *The Beardsley Period* (1925). Much like Murdoch and Muddiman before him, Burdett limits his representative autumnal group to Beardsley, Wilde, Symons, Johnson, Dowson, Le Gallienne, Beerbohm, Davidson, and Crackanthorpe, the young men in a protesting mood, "a mood of excess natural to youthful imagination." The sources Burdett cites for this movement, Flaubert, Baudelaire, and Zola, suggest once more the interrelationship of the several tendencies of the time.

Burdett opens the crucial fourth chapter, on "The Last Decade," with a long quotation from H. G. Wells's *The Story of a Great Schoolmaster* (1924), in which Wells describes the 1880s as having "a delusive air of final establishment" but beneath whose "tranquil-looking surfaces many ferments were actively at work." Burdett places the emphasis on the "air of final establishment" rather than on "ferment." However, in order to argue that the nineties represent the last spurt of energy of the last Victorians or the last romantics, Burdett must eliminate those talents "which had not been born under the romantic star, talents contemporaneously stirring vital currents, breaking new ground, inventing new motives in place of refining upon the old, with an eye turned not to the past, but to the future." He excludes those who "were endeavoring to create a new synthesis of belief." Among these, Burdett lists Wells, Shaw, Kipling, and Bennett. But this is to ignore the twelve to fourteen principal works Wells had published before 1900, not to mention journalism; it is to dismiss a very considerable amount of the early work of Shaw; and it is at least to ignore what Bennett owed to the spirit of the eighties and nineties and to George Moore specifically. Moore, Gissing, Hardy, the early Yeats, and many others are relatively slighted because they apparently do not fit conveniently into the group of young men who died young. With the need to eliminate so much one wonders whether the nineties have any claim to being called the Beardsley period.

This special group, according to Burdett, is held together by its respect for contemporary "foreign, particularly French, movements" and by the fact that it was "oblivious of the English currents of its own time because they were scientific or social or coldly intellectual." Burdett then suggests that the *fin de siècle* group has a sense of disillusion "that can never dominate a pioneer." If these statements do nothing else, they should at least challenge someone to write a dissertation on the scientific interests of the men of the nineties, especially Francis Thompson's; the scholarly intellectual quality of Lionel Johnson's mind is already too well known to warrant comment; and the social interests of Oscar Wilde and others are also apparent.

My survey of the writings about the nineties published up to about 1925 seems to lead to two conclusions. First, the nineties were generally regarded either as a self-sufficient movement, beginning in 1890 and ending in 1900, or only as the ending of something which started much earlier. Secondly, the various characteristics of the nineties were commonly forced under the single label of decadence, for which the more general term "romanticism" is sometimes substituted. These two conclusions I would now like to examine while I lead you back to my original thesis of a period describable as a time of experimentation and transition.

I have omitted from my discussion two pertinent books published before 1926: Holbrook Jackson's *The Eighteen Nineties* (1913) and Richard Le Gallienne's *The Romantic Nineties* (1925). Both books differ from the works I have referred to in that, despite Le Gallienne's title, neither work falls into the fallacy of the simplified label. Jackson's book is distinguished from others by its inclusiveness, its broad sympathy (without defensiveness) for *all* aspects of the period, and its recognition of the fact that the period was not formed by its books and pictures only but by political and social changes as well.[31] He also gives more space to Wells and Shaw than most previous writers, who generally do not mention Wells at all; he does not dismiss Moore as a man of the eighties who happened to write a few books in the nineties before he disappeared into the Celtic literary movement; Jackson at least mentions Hardy a dozen times, though the references come to little enough; he recognizes the importance of William Archer and the drama generally; he recognizes the importance of the early Yeats and of William Sharp; and he rescues many minor talents from oblivion without exaggerating their quality of influence. On the other hand, even in Jackson there is practically nothing on the humorists, Barry Pain, Jerome K. Jerome, Pett Ridge, and others; there is too little or nothing on Arthur Waugh, an important defender of the tradition, Andrew Lang, Frederic Harrison, Clement K. Shorter, editor of some of the most characteristic papers and periodicals of the time, Vernon Lee, and many more; and while the French influence on the literature of the time gets its due, Russian literature is rather slighted, even though the periodicals issued during the thirteen years before Jackson's book appeared contained many articles on the influence of Russian literature. In more recent years the tendency to overemphasize the French influence and to slight the Russian has been somewhat corrected, as in some of the work of Clarence Decker, Harold Orel, Royal A. Gettmann, and Gilbert Phelps.

While Jackson tends to emphasize the French influence, he does not exaggerate the importance of decadence, especially in its sensational aspect, nor does he underrate it as mere stylistic idiosyncrasy or an uninfluential chaos of debased ideas. He recognizes its relationship with the earlier romanticism, even with classicism, with the naturalistic movement, and with the slightly later symbolist movement. The book is perhaps best summed up in the words Jackson, at the end, applies to the black-and-white art of the time:

> In the work of no single artist was a final interpretation of reality attained. The art of the time was perhaps too personal for that; just as it was too personal for work within prescribed conventions and formalities. The age favoured experiment and adventure. . . . In this large tolerance the spirit of renaissance worked through mind and imagination inspiring artists with a new confidence in themselves and courage to take risks.

Le Gallienne's book also takes a broader view of the period's characteristics. For him the nineties is a period of transition in which three generations are actively in being. He suggests the idea of continuity, of new departures, of the meeting of conflicting ideas, and the blending of tradition and experiment. Le Gallienne gives a more balanced view of the period than most writers, who were dazzled with delight or blinded with disgust by one or the other aspect of the time.[32] "It is always misleading as it is tempting," he warns us, "to compress a period into a formula, and to find for it a 'spirit' in which its expressive figures are supposed to participate. . . ."[33] In writing of Davidson, Symons, Henley, and others, Le Gallienne seems to be praising a subtle blending of aestheticism, decadence, and realism which he refers to as "imaginative realism."[34] S. C. Roberts, in his more recent essay, "At the Heart of the Nineties," which is essentially a review of the year 1894, also shows that the period is no more decadent than it is any one of a number of other things.

This writer reminds us that "literary wild oats are sown in every generation," and he concludes that "the fertile and varied output of such a year as 1894 remains an impressive token of literary vitality." [35]

It should now be apparent that the nineties, much less still the period from 1870 to 1930, are not identical with the aesthetic movement or the decadent movement or even the still more vaguely defined romantic movement.[36] Historians of the period in general and even those studying but one movement have, since about 1925, adopted a more flexible approach than earlier writers. They have recognized that the period was not a period of several unrelated or necessarily antithetical movements, and they have begun to affirm that the various movements discoverable in the nineties did not die with the nineties. Thus, even in Holbrook Jackson's cautious wording, the nineties end in "a retreat—but not a defeat." Thus, Mario Praz, in tracing one aspect of romanticism through the nineteenth century, holds that "it would have been easy to trace the course of certain currents of the Decadent period right down to the present day," that is to 1933.[37] Similarly, Louise Rosenblatt [38] recognizes the complex interrelations of the several artistic movements associated with the last two decades of the nineteenth century, and in her conclusion suggests that the art-for-art's-sake point of view is one of the major characteristic tendencies of the eclectic twentieth century. It would be instructive to consider what the early work of Evelyn Waugh and Aldous Huxley owes directly to the French decadents as well as to the modified English version of the movement. For that matter, there is much in the work of D. H. Lawrence, James Joyce, and other later writers that recalls decadent literature with, perhaps, some support from the newer developments in psychology and psychoanalysis.

What I have been saying about decadence, aestheticism, and young-manism applies as well to naturalism as a characterizing movement of the period. The essentials of the debate between Arthur Waugh and Hubert Crackanthorpe in the *Yellow Book* and of the battle over Zola's work did not end with the nineties. The announcement in the *Catholic World* (June, 1895) of Zola's downfall was premature. The old naturalism of sociological man in part becomes the new realism of psychological man, as Arthur Waugh himself recognized.[39] Walter L. Myers, however, in *The Later Realism* (1927) shows in more detail the connection between late nineteenth-century naturalism and early twentieth-century realism. Thus, the novelists of his Group III (May Sinclair, Lawrence, Rebecca West, Dorothy Richardson, Joyce [40]), "whose work contains the clearest instances of incongruity and extra-realism in characterization," have been influenced not only by Freudian psychology but by the general revolt against Victorian prudery

> which as an importation from France, begins with Swinburne and others in a sort of artistic baiting of the commonplace respectability, becomes by the turn of the century a strong force of social criticism, gains momentum by the growing interest in genetics, and rises to a crest in the general disintegration of the older way of life following the world-war.[41]

The work of the writers in Myers's Group II (Bennett, Galsworthy, and Wells) shows similar connections with the late nineteenth-century search for truth and greater freedom in the technique and content of imaginative literature.[42]

Clarence Decker, in his *PMLA* article in 1938, "The Aesthetic Revolt against Naturalism in Victorian Criticism," records the softening of the moral objectors, as in the case of Robert Buchanan, and describes the aesthetic attack on naturalism. However, what we actually witness in the criticism of J. A. Symonds, Lang, Meredith, Stevenson, Moore, Wilde, and Arthur Symons is not a rejection of naturalism but a modification of the French movement under various influences: romance (in Lang, Symonds, Meredith, and Stevenson), the Russian novelists (in Moore's contrast of the fact-mind of Zola and the thought-mind of Turgenev), even of the art-for-art's-sake theory (in Wilde's contrasting Balzac's "imaginative realism" and Zola's "unimaginative realism"), and of impressionism and symbolism (in Arthur Symons's work). Thus, naturalism having in the eighties and nineties undergone various modifications, Decker can conclude that these changes are "partially responsible for the deflection of Naturalism into the numerous subjective Realisms of late nineteenth and early twentieth century fiction." William C. Frierson has also insisted that the nineties witnessed not so much the genesis or the demise of a particular movement as the modification of that movement to suit the English temper, a marriage of French theories with the English tradition. In Frierson's *The English Novel in Transition: 1885–1940* (1942) naturalism, subdivided into the Zolaesque kind and Huysmans's "spiritualistic naturalism," with George Moore as the catalyst, becomes the unifying element of the period which began in the 1880s and continued to about 1930.

The coherence and unity of the broad, complex period of which the nineties is only a small part are also described by other post-1930 writers. Janko Lavrin in *Aspects of Modernism, from Wilde to Pirandello* (1935) discusses both Wilde and Lawrence against the broad background of the " 'new' European sensibility." Lavrin writes: "Utter atomization of the individual, and parallel with this, a passionate though impotent will to achieve at least some balance and harmony in spite of all—such are the two polar trends reflected in European modernism as a whole." This generalization Lavrin illustrates by suggesting that despite his flirting with a state beyond good and evil, Oscar Wilde was "a latent moralist in whom the moral instinct had been either suppressed or else deprived too early of an adequate will and outlet," that Wilde had a glimpse that self-indulgence "was but a poor substitute for self-realization." [43] Lavrin's comment recalls a similar one by Edwin Bjorkman on Galsworthy.[44] Bjorkman maintains that Galsworthy's art above all gives the impression of modernity, of "a time between two ages," a time of "a vain struggle to reach stability between a dying and a coming faith—between the faith in authority, in the god-given destiny of 'the best men,' and the faith in voluntary service and the intrinsic worth of all normal men." Bjorkman, in trying to find an appropriate label to describe Galsworthy's art, hits upon one not unlike Oscar Wilde's "imaginative realism" as a label for Balzac's art. Galsworthy's art, Bjorkman says, m y best be described by such new synthesizing terms as "symbolical impressionism" or "spiritual realism." Synthesis of a similar kind is also evident in the *art nouveau,* which is a significant expression of the transition from the nineteenth to the twentieth century. According to S. T. Madsen,[45] the sources of this movement are the arts and crafts movement, Pre-Raphaelitism, and the symbolist movement. J. Gordon Eaker has also described "emergent modernism" as a complex synthesis of many artistic and social currents. Among others, Eaker lists the tendency to substitute adjustment to the world for escape from it, a new interest in nature, the distrust of reason and greater emphasis on the unconscious mind and instinct, greater freedom for women, the tendency to break the compromise between the aristocracy and the middle class, and the trend toward pragmatism and the experimental attitude.[46]

Still other writers have discovered the causes of this transitional period in social developments. Thus, A. J. Philip makes much of "the education of the masses . . . that made the 'Golden Period' possible" and argues that the story of transition from 1870 to 1920 "is largely one of the emergence of truth and her reburial."[47] According to Philip, the period begins under the stimulus of the emerging factory system, the rise of the mechanics institutes, and the influence of such legislation as the Education Act of 1870, and it ends with the effects of the First World War and the decline of educational standards. H. V. Routh, in *Towards the Twentieth Century* (1937), also finds that social causation, although more broadly cultural in kind than that proposed by Philip, accounts for the transition at the end of the century. The transition for Routh chiefly involves the clash between "culture," industrial civilization, and science. Granville Hicks, writing from a Marxist point of view in *Figures in Transition* (1939), also ascribes the late Victorian *Zeitgeist* to social-economic causes.

One of the more recent general works on the period from 1880 on to recognize its complexity and to point out the continuity of its many divergent movements is William York Tindall's *Forces in Modern British Literature: 1885–1946* (1947; rev. ed., 1956). According to Tindall, within the larger framework of romanticism, the period from about 1885 on "constitutes a whole," and the characteristics of this whole are implicit in the literature of the 1880s. Thus, aestheticism and decadence can be traced from Wilde to Joyce; so, also, the Zola tradition, the symbolist tradition, the detailed revelation of the conscious mind resulting in the stream-of-consciousness technique, the exploration of the unconscious, and new impulses toward mythology emanating from the new anthropology and psychology can all be traced through the entire period, and all contributed to the temper and continuity of the period.

Tindall's comprehensive study is too wide in scope to permit adequate study in detail of many specific problems that still need examination. However, a few specialized studies published during the 1930s and 1940s help to provide some of the details, as, for example, the examination of popular literature from 1887 to 1914 by Malcolm Elwin in *Old Gods Falling* (1939) and Amy Cruse's more reliable but inadequately documented book, *After the Victorians* (1938), on the same period and much the same subject. George H. Ford's *Dickens and His Readers* (1955) and Richard D. Altick's *The English Common Reader . . . , 1800–1900* (1957), while both books only set foot lightly into the period with which I am concerned, contribute much to our understanding of previously slighted areas. Ruth Temple's *The Critic's Alchemy: A Study of the Introduction of French Symbolism into England* (1953) does much to lay the groundwork for further studies of the criticism of Arthur Symons, Sir Edmund Gosse,

George Moore and others. From 1932 on there has been a spate of books and articles on symbolism after about 1910 but still little on the English symbolist movement from 1880 to 1900; there have been chiefly French, German, and Italian works on the decadent movement in England; and we have been inundated with articles and books on the post-romantic romantic movement.

In reviewing the commentaries on the question of the characteristics of the nineties, I elected to begin by noting an emphasis on decadence variously modified by relational references to aestheticism, naturalism, and symbolism. I might have begun with any of the other movements and said much the same thing. These are some of the specific movements that characterize not only the nineties but the entire period from about 1870 to about 1930. But they are movements that cannot be isolated in separate pigeonholes. If they are not separable, one might ask, on what ground do they overlap? Do they have anything in common? Do they cumulatively help us to reach some general conclusions about the characteristics of the period in which they occurred? These movements seem to me to overlap in three general areas: (1) the relationship of artist to audience, (2) the relationship of the work of art to the traditional concepts of truth and reality, and (3) the relationship of the work of art to the mood, the point of view of the time.

First, all these movements assert the authority of the artist, his superiority to his audience. The tendency to divorce morality from art is significant. "Freedom," "the break with tradition," and "the death of Mrs. Grundy" are frequently sounded tunes. The result, as often in a period of experimentation, was increased isolation of the artist from the mass reading public. Thus, David Daiches [48] can write of "the breakdown of communities of belief," especially in connection with aestheticism and symbolism, and can declare that "the 1890's saw a shift in the poet's conception of his own function from that of a public figure to a private one"; and Melvin Rader can write of "The Artist as Outsider." [49]

Secondly, all these movements attempted a reassessment of what constitutes truth in art and in life. Thus, against those who believed that truth is absolute and not subject to radical redefinition, the artists from 1880 on, the "determined disquieters" (an epithet applied to Ibsen), insisted on reinterpreting objective, external truth, sociological and biological truth; others insisted on penetrating subjective, psychological truth beyond the barriers that had been established. Nor was this a mere echo of similar activity in earlier stages of man's cultural history. The new science of sociology, the developing science of psychology, new concepts in physics, mathematics, and biology had changed the terms of the discussion. If one recalls the Vizetelly trials, Oscar Wilde's trial, the debate between Wells and Henry James, the debate between Arthur Waugh and Hubert Crackanthorpe, the debate between Wells–Bennett–Galsworthy group and the Virginia Woolf–Dorothy Richardson group, the attacks on and the defenses of D. H. Lawrence, and James Joyce's publication difficulties, there is little doubt that this battle for artistic truth and truth about life was one of the most dramatic of the period from 1870 to about 1930. [50]

Thirdly, and closely related to the preceding two aspects of the period, through all these movements there can be heard a note of melancholy.[51] While the mood is an ancient and often recurrent one, the immediate stimuli for it between 1870 and 1930 were the events that give the period its historical individuality. It is the melancholy that results from the concurrent "dash for life" and the apparent longing for death, from the coexistence of the sense of ending and beginning, from the regret for the passing aristocratic leadership and the hope for the leadership of everyman, from the concurrent desire for Little England and peace and for Empire and the rigors of the struggle to maintain imperial grandeur. We may, therefore, after all speak of the last Victorians, but in the same breath we must also speak of the first moderns. This is why we must speak of journeys out, but not out of senile Victorianism into brash but arid Modernism. The transition is from one fertile land into another, and the transition is itself through a fertile land.

III

In view of this vast sea of print about the nineties and their environs, what remains to be said in the future? The quantity of writing about the period is misleading, for much of it is repetitive or sensational and unreliable. Vast gaps in scholarship still remain. Some of these gaps are in process of being filled.[52] However, a survey of several major bibliographies back to 1930 suggests that much fundamental work still needs to be done.

Since very few of Moore's and Glissing's novels are readily available in America, reprints, or better, modern editions of at least three or four by each are a fundamental requirement; among the works of lesser writers, it would be useful to have easily available editions of at least the best work of the following: Arthur Morrison, Israel Zangwill, Mark Rutherford, Walter Besant (especially the *Autobiography*), Richard Whiteing, Leonard Merrick, Maurice Hewlett, and at least some of the comic novels and stories of Pett Ridge, Jerome K. Jerome, and Barry Pain. Poets like John Davidson, Lionel Johnson, and Francis Thompson are, in my opinion, not adaquately represented in even the more specialized anthologies, a lacuna which can probably only be filled by a really fresh anthology of the poetry from about 1880 to 1920.

Most neglected, except for those of Shaw, Yeats, Hardy, and, recently, Moore and Gissing, have been solid critical studies of most of the writers of the period. Especially needed are major critical studies of Wilde as poet and critic; of Francis Thompson, whose literary criticism was collected by T. L. Connolly in 1948; of Vernon Lee, whose papers are now at Colby College and whose critical writings deserve more attention than they have had; and a full-scale critical study of Lionel Johnson. We also need sympathetic studies of such critics as William Archer, Andrew Lang, and Edmund Gosse. Walter Besant, whose *Autobiography* Walter Houghton seems to have rediscovered, deserves some attention for his comments on the art of fiction.[53]

We also still need objective scholarly biographies of Oscar Wilde, George Moore, Gissing, Davidson, and many lesser writers; we could do nicely with a thorough critical study of the English short story during this period; we should welcome further studies of the serious drama of the time; we need a study of the comic novel of the period; and many characteristic periodicals of the period also still need to be studied. The last word has undoubtedly not been said on the major literary movements of the period, but I should especially like to see more attention given to their interrelationship and their reflection in works after 1900. This, I suspect, can only be done when more scholars have stopped thinking of the year 1900 as marking the dead end of a literary cult.

Equally urgent is the need for a new revaluation of the entire period, a book which would thoroughly review the scholarship of the past fifty years, which would take into consideration the many valuable foreign works on the period, and which would consider *de novo* the major writers and literary movements of the period. This kind of synthesis has become possible because the restless forces that began in about 1870, gathered momentum in the 1880s, and regrouped in the 1890s and early years of the twentieth century, had by about 1930 slackened. Meeting the challenge which can result in a renaissance of scholarship on the nineties and their environs is the opportunity of all who are convinced, as I am, that the nineties are not merely a vestigial organ dragging along in the shadow of the Victorian period.

᷂

W. B. Yeats: History and the Shaping Joy

THOMAS R. WHITAKER

We need not ask what Yeats would retort if accused of being an Edwardian. Remember his disdainful allusion to "new commonness / Upon the throne and crying about the streets." But "In the Seven Woods" itself may remind us that he was entering a crucial period. He was turning from a poetry of "vision" to one of "drama." He no longer sought impersonal essences of truth and beauty; he sought the "wisdom of the body." He said in 1903 that the moment of "Transfiguration" had yielded to the moment of "Incarnation," the yearning Dionysian to the self-sufficient Apollonian. As in himself, so in history: "I feel about me and in me an impulse to create form. . . ."[1] He later called it the subjective or *antithetical* impulse, which may find its bounding outline or satirical edge by opposing the *primary* nature of its time, the "new commonness" symbolized by Edward's coronation. And as Yeats obeyed that impulse, his work grew tougher, saltier, more ironic, and more arrogant.

Behind that change we may glimpse many apparent causes: the exhaustion of the literary movement of the nineties, the transformation of Ireland by the rising middle classes, the marriage of Maud Gonne, Yeats's friendship with Lady Gregory, his writing plays and defending plays, and all the "Theatre business, management of men," which made his Pegasus

> Shiver under the lash, strain, sweat and jolt
> As though it dragged road-metal.

But those were occasions, opportunities. Yeats knew that the springs of action are found within. The title of that poem about Pegasus is clear enough: "The Fascination of What's Difficult." Though not yet part of the complete doctrine of the "Mask," that fascination was far from new. Yeats's career had long been based upon a dialogue with his opposite—upon a criticism of the existing self and an exploration of what he called "that dark portion of the mind which is like the other side of the moon." [2] "Rosa Alchemica," for example, dramatizes the dark forces that later destroyed its own Pateresque style; and its conception of spiritual alchemy shows that in 1896 Yeats already saw "Transfiguration" as but a preliminary stage in his own alchemical "Great Work."

In general, he understood that Great Work as a dialectical progress of the soul through the opposites toward ever greater completeness. During the Edwardian period he stressed, and his critics have continued to stress, its Apollonian aspect: the "search for more of manful energy, more of cheerful acceptance of whatever arises out of the logic of events, and for clean outline." [3] But we must ask: If his reversal was really an exploratory shift of emphasis, what had happened to the qualities dominant in his earlier work? Increasingly he wrote of the cycles of history, of the individual's action within time and subjection to time. What had happened to his early longing for freedom in contemplation, for an apocalyptic transcendence of time? Increasingly he was aristocratic, contemptuous, violent. What had happened to his early ideals of equality, charity, and peace? The answers to these questions may shed some light on that period when Yeats was becoming not only his own tragic character but also one of the most profoundly ethical poets of our time.

I

It is symptomatic that in his prose meditations upon Apollonian qualities within history, Yeats's imagination still tended to move quite beyond history. In 1904 he described those qualities as created by the "high disciplined or individual kingly mind," the "measurer-out" or "marker-in of limits," which he called "solar" —though it became "lunar" in his later system. But such art, he said, brings "not merely discipline but joy; for its discipline is . . . the expression of the individual soul turning itself into a pure fire and imposing its own pattern, its own music, upon the heaviness and dumbness that is in others and in itself." In the moment of self-expression, the artist transcends the external and objective pressures of his time. History is consumed in his pure fire. Again in 1908 Yeats said that such art cannot come "until a public opinion is ready to welcome in the mind of the artist a power, little affected by external things, being self-contained, self-created, self-sufficing." Then, at "the instant of revelation, writers think the world is but their palette, and if history amuses them, it is but, as Goethe says, because they would do its personages the honour of naming after them their own thoughts." But this transcendence of history is not just a matter of subjective individualism. As his term "revelation" suggests, Yeats believed the Apollonian impulse to have a universal or even transcendental basis. Therefore it might lead men toward a social Unity of Being. In 1909 he praised the Greek canon of beauty as evidence of a "compact between the artist and society." Greek statues, like the work of Dürer ten centuries later, seemed to celebrate a "resurrection into unity"[4]—and in that phrase Yeats evoked the apocalyptic goal of Blake's poetry, the reconstitution of the un-fallen Adam and his paradisal world.

So it was whenever Yeats celebrated life in time. He suggested that poets "discover thoughts that tighten the muscles, or quiver and tingle in the flesh"—but his sentence then became apocalyptic—"and so stand like St. Michael with the trumpet that calls the body to resurrection." He said that Greek art, if carried to its logical conclusion, would gather up "by a kind of deification a capacity for all energy and all passion, into a Krishna, a Christ, a Dionysus."[5] As he imagines the Apollonian form, it is so filled with the energy Blake called "eternal delight" that it becomes Dionysian. Clearly, the ultimate goal of the "measurer-out" is to pass beyond all measurement. The bounded is a way toward the boundless. But this is not the yearning transcendence of Yeats's early poetry; it is the joyful transcendence of formal accomplishment and of energy in excess.

Nor did Yeats imagine it as occurring only at ideal moments in history. A similar movement of thought appears in his discussions of present conflicts and defeats. In 1904, after describing the death of our civilization, he progressively postponed the new era of history until it seemed to enter the realm of myth. And as he did so, his hope for a specific future event became a confidence in the present heroic potential of man. "Every argument," he could then say, "carries us back to some religious conception, and in the end the creative energy of men depends upon their believing that they have, within themselves, something immortal and imperishable, and that all else is but an image in a looking-glass." And at the end of this essay, when praising art that cele-brates the active personality, he used images that suggest temporal defeat and transcendental victory: "when Lucifer stands among his friends, when Villon sings his dead ladies to so gallant a rhythm, when Timon makes his epitaph, we feel no sorrow, for life herself has made one of her eternal gestures, has called up into our hearts her energy that is eternal delight." [6]

This statement recalls Nietzsche's view that in Greek tragedy the boundless Dionysian celebration of eternal life arises amid the defeat of the Apollonian hero, who is but an individual vessel of that life. But Nietzsche was clarifying for Yeats a position that Yeats himself had long held. Many years before, the Ellis and Yeats study of Blake had stated that "incarnation and crucifixion . . . are identical." When Christ or the poetic genius enters time, it becomes subject to the conflicts and defeats symbolized by the cross. Moreover, "Christ put on the temporal body, which is Satan, on purpose that it might be consumed, and the 'spiritual body revealed.'" [7] For exactly the same purpose, during the Edwardian period Yeats's own poetic genius began to put on the temporal body. His earlier understanding of "Transfiguration" had been hasty and immature. One must fully enter time before transcending it. One must create form before transfiguring it.

In the Blake study Yeats had said that "We must cast our life, thought after thought, desire after desire," into the imagination's "world of freedom, and so escape from the warring egotisms of elements and years." But he had spoken too much like a weary aesthete. After the turn of the century, discovering that life must be fully lived before it is cast away, he developed that theory somewhat in the direction of Schopenhauer, with whose work and whose Vedic sources he had long had some acquaintance. For Schopenhauer the "only event-in-itself" is the "assertion and denial of the will to live, when self-consciousness has been attained." For Yeats, as in *At the Hawk's Well,* that is no final choice but a tension:

> The heart would be always awake,
> The heart would turn to its rest.

The Phoenix nest upon the Tree of Life, he said, holds "the passion that is exaltation and the negation of the will." But Schopenhauer also considered that double consciousness to belong to the poet, as distinct from the saint. In fact, he saw the poet as so becoming his own tragic character. Contemplating and reproducing the drama of life, while bearing its cost himself, the poet might attain the "sublime"—which occurs when, "in the undismayed beholder, the twofold nature of his consciousness reaches the highest degree of distinctness," and he perceives himself both "as an individual, . . . the frail phenomenon of will," and "as the eternal, peaceful, knowing subject . . . free and apart from all desires and necessities." [8]

In 1922 Yeats described most clearly his own version of that tragic sublimity, attained by poets for whom "contemplation" is no escape from life but "the worst crisis of all." Dante and Villon, he said, "would not, when they speak through their art, change their luck; yet they are mirrored in all the suffering of desire. The two halves of their nature are so completely joined that they seem to labour for their objects, and yet to desire whatever happens, being at the same instant predestinate and free, creation's very self." But Yeats implied a creative and unified acceptance of life that is foreign to Schopenhauer. The poet may so discover or release within himself a cosmic creativity, a "shaping joy"—as Yeats described it in 1907—which delights in nothing more than to fuse in a single image both Will and Mask, both history and its transcendence. "This joy," he said, "because it must be always making and mastering, remains in the hands and in the tongue of the artist, but with his eyes he enters upon a submissive, sorrowful contemplation of the great irremediable things. . . ." [9]

Presenting this view in Rosicrucian terms, Yeats described the Rose no longer as the sorrowful wandering beauty which, like the Shekinah or Presence of God, suffers with man the woes of a fallen world, but as the ecstasy known when one's private fate and the world itself are transcended in tragic art. The last words of Timon and Cleopatra move us, he said, "because their sorrow is not their own at tomb or asp, but for all men's fate. That shaping joy has kept the sorrow pure. . . ." In other words, the artist's creative delight has enabled him to escape morbid self-preoccupation, to balance every motive with its hidden opposite, and so to attain an objective vision of the generic tragedy of life. For "the nobleness of the Arts," Yeats continued, "is in the mingling of contraries, the extremity of sorrow, the extremity of joy, perfection of personality, the perfection of its surrender, overflowing turbulent energy, and marmorean stillness; and its red rose opens at the meeting of the two beams of the cross, and at the trysting-place of time and eternity." [10] Such art weds the Apollonian and the Dionysian. It puts on and consumes the temporal body; it accepts and transcends history. Its ecstasy arises from three sources: the artist's joy in experiencing our limited temporal life; his joy in contemplating it, amid defeat, as an "eternal gesture" of "life herself"; and his "shaping joy," which has enabled him to bring to a single focus those contrary joys in the bounded and the boundless. Yeats called such art "tragic"; but his stress upon its joy indicates his continuing belief that the profoundest tragedy points, however obscurely, toward a universal or divine comedy.

II

But how does such a contemplative transcendence of time, no facile escape but an agonizing and joyful crisis, begin to enter Yeats's poetic work? Characters in his plays occasionally describe that "tragic joy" which, he said in 1904, reaches its climax "when the world itself has slipped away in death." [11] The poet of *The King's Threshold* proclaims that "when all falls / In ruin, poetry calls out in joy." And Yeats reworked *The Shadowy Waters* until he could say in 1905 that it was "now upon one single idea —which is in these new lines—

> 'When the world ends
> The mind is made unchanging for it finds
> Miracle, ecstasy, the impossible joy,
> The flagstone under all, the fire of fires,
> The root of the world.' "

But, he added, the play "is only right in its highest moments—the logic and circumstances are all wrong." [12] Though he began to invent such circumstances for his plays, his lyric poems show more clearly his progress toward realizing in "minute particulars" those insights which he could now put abstractly.

His first problem, which has received most critical attention, was that of developing a language to render action in the temporal world. But there was also the problem of transcending that world, of moving from "Incarnation" to "Transfiguration," from the "circling necessity" to free contemplation. "Adam's Curse" is one early attempt to present such a movement. Critics have often praised its vigorous conversational idiom—

> Better go down upon your marrow-bones
> And scrub a kitchen pavement, or break stones
> Like an old pauper, in all kinds of weather

—and have also noted that its conclusion strangely lapses into an earlier diction:

> We saw the last embers of daylight die,
> And in the trembling blue-green of the sky
> A moon, worn as if it had been a shell
> Washed by time's waters as they rose and fell
> About the stars and broke in days and years.

But, whatever its success, that is not a lapse but a strategy. The poem rises through an everyday scene, which is "solar," to a "lunar" contemplative moment, in which the meaning of that scene emerges as the curse of a time-bound world: "we'd grown / As weary-hearted as that hollow moon." In 1902 Yeats's new vigor was mainly limited to rendering action in time; he still had no contemplative diction but that of a melancholy, yearning transfiguration, with its lunar "emotion of multitude." [13]

In two versions of "Red Hanrahan's Song about Ireland" we can see him shifting from such a passive transcendence to a more active one. The 1894 song, almost reversing the effect of Mangan's martial refrain, seems to describe a flight from the world of action to a contemplative refuge:

> Weak and worn and weary the waves of Cummen Strand,
> When the wind comes blowing across the hilly land;
> Weak and worn and weary our courage droops and dies
> But our hearts are lighted from the flame in the eyes
> Of Kathleen-Ny-Hoolihan.

By 1903, however, that flight became an active surmounting of defeat. Though the speaker is broken, a joyous defiance rings in his words, and his transcendence seems to result from a snatching and hiding of the flame. His soul is turning itself into a "pure fire."

> The old brown thorn trees break in two high over Cummen
>   Strand
> Under a bitter black wind that blows from the left hand,
> Our courage breaks like an old tree in a black wind and dies;
> But we have hidden in our hearts the flame out of the eyes
> Of Cathleen, the daughter of Houlihan.

On such broken thorn-trees, in the later "Meditations in Time of Civil War," Yeats would hope for the "symbolic rose" to "break in flower." But Joyce's Stephen Dedalus did not need to wait until 1923 to recognize and endorse this as the language of Yeats's tragic joy and artistic creativity. On that semi-fictional June 16, 1904, he gave its Blakean and Rosicrucian correlaries: "Know all men, he said, time's ruins build eternity's mansions. What means this? Desire's wind blasts the thorntree but after it becomes from a bramble bush to be a rose upon the rood of time." [14]

Yeats's next problem was to infuse the contemplative moment with yet more energy or, conversely, to infuse the soul's action and passion with contemplation. The poem must not end with a detachable tag of lunar reverie or even a detachable flame from Cathleen's eyes. Like the Apollonian statue, it must contain within its limited form of an action both "marmorean stillness" and "overflowing turbulent energy."

"No Second Troy," a poem of 1908, approaches that goal. It is a passionate utterance, almost the speaker's argument with himself, yet the dominant voice is that of detachment and acceptance:

> Why should I blame her that she filled my days
> With misery, or that she would of late
> Have taught to ignorant men most violent ways,
> Or hurled the little streets upon the great,
> Had they but courage equal to desire?

The passion to blame is increasingly submerged—with the effect of Lear's "Hysterica passio, down, thou climbing sorrow!"—until the poem explodes in its last fiery question: "Was there another Troy for her to burn?" Though the beloved seems vindicated, we do not forget that "counter-truth," that passion being kept down by the sword's point.[15] The very hyperbole of praise uttered by the voice of acceptance includes all that the *hysterica passio* might say against this destructive Helen. The rhetorically triumphant question fully reveals the submerged wound. Like Dante or Villon, Yeats's speaker still seems to labor for his object though accepting, even desiring, whatever happens. The exultant tone of the conclusion partly arises, then, from the wedding of the active and contemplative halves of the self. And because the "shaping joy" has kept the sorrow pure, the speaker's utterance reveals, like his beloved's actions, "a mind / That nobleness made simple as a fire," though with a hidden tension that gives it "beauty like a tightened bow." Here, as in many later poems, the speaker incarnates in his own defeat the nobility he sees in the defeated person upon whom he meditates. His transcendence of time and hers become one.

A similar though quieter effect occurs in "Against Unworthy Praise"; but Yeats soon developed more forceful ways of charging the moment of contemplation and transcending the limited historical action. In "Friends," a poem of 1911, the dispassionate voice of judgment, finally overwhelmed, can do no more than describe the speaker's own passionate state:

> up from my heart's root
> So great a sweetness flows
> I shake from head to foot.

The final words evoke an image of the limited physical body, which has been charged with an excess of energy and delight. By 1912, in "The Cold Heaven," Yeats translated the entire moment of contemplation into an overwhelming vision: "Suddenly I saw the cold and rook-delighting heaven. . . ." The slight distancing effect of the past tense disappears in the final cry:

> Ah! When the ghost begins to quicken,
> Confusion of the death-bed over, is it sent
> Out naked on the roads, as the books say, and stricken
> By the injustice of the skies for punishment?

Again the limited body—now the naked "spiritual body" revealed by incarnation and crucifixion—is "Riddled with light." In 1913 "The Magi" used a similar technique to develop material drawn from a less personal history. The vision's intensity here derives from its hallucinatory permanence ("Now as at all times I can see in the mind's eye"), from its hardness (the "stiff, painted clothes" of the Magi, their "faces like rain-beaten stones"), and from its movement away from those disillusioned images of yearning "Transfiguration" toward the unconscious animal force they lack: "The uncontrollable mystery on the bestial floor." And in that final line, the solidly limited is again transfigured by an excessive energy.

But as Yeats dramatized the active man on the stage of history, his problem of contemplative transcendence became yet more acute. How can one write topical verse, in which the speaker argues not with himself but with others, and yet remain true to the belief that art disengages the soul from history? The rhetorical attack itself must be purged by the "shaping joy," as in the Gaelic poet's curse where "delight in . . . vehemence," Yeats said in 1910, has taken "out of anger half the bitterness with all the gloom." The poet's joy may keep him from being psychologically dependent upon those whom he attacks. As Yeats said of the Irish, "Our minds, being sufficient to themselves, do not wish for victory but are content to elaborate our extravagance, if fortune aid, into wit or lyric beauty." The root motive of such a poetic elaboration is neither hatred of an opponent nor desire for social change, but love of a transcendent ideal, an "impossibly noble life." Its "core," as Yeats said of all great art, is "an over-powering vision of certain virtues, and our capacity for sharing in that vision is the measure of our delight." [16]

So it is, for example, in Yeats's poem of 1909 "Upon a House Shaken by the Land Agitation." The title itself, with a touch of irony, universalizes the topical. And in the first quatrain that house almost disappears in the impossibly noble life it has nourished:

> How should the world be luckier if this house,
> Where passion and precision have been one
> Time out of mind, became too ruinous
> To breed the lidless eye that loves the sun?

We have moved from the present fact to a vision of an endless history, and then to a vision of an eternal virtue—that high disciplined mind symbolized by eagle's eye and sun. Then, amplifying that movement, the poem adds sweetness to strength:

> And the sweet laughing eagle thoughts that grow
> Where wings have memory of wings, and all
> That comes of the best knit to the best? Although
> Mean roof-trees were the sturdier for its fall,
> How should their luck run high enough to reach

> The gifts that govern men, and after these
> To gradual Time's last gift, a written speech
> Wrought of high laughter, loveliness and ease?

Here again the conclusion has a strange depth: that high climax, the goal at the end of Time, shaken by temporal agitation yet clearly transcending it, is the "written speech" of this poem itself. Its "loveliness and ease" have almost refined away the thought of political argument. The speaker does not "wish for victory"; his graceful questions elaborate his vision of "certain virtues." And we are not tempted to quarrel about whether those virtues have appeared in a particular Irish house; rather, we delightedly share in that vision.

"September 1913" is yet more successful in transcending its occasion, because of the far richer use of the speaker's own personality as its final meaning. This is most evident in its conclusion. One critic has said that "although the poem as a whole is the record of a man's imagined attempt to use all the devices of speech, from conversation to oratory, in the effort to inculcate a point of view," the "end of the effort is a satiric taunt that would hardly attain its aim." [17] But that is exactly the point. Never is the speaker's mind really upon "victory"—and let's recall that last stanza in detail:

> Yet could we turn the years again,
> And call those exiles as they were
> In all their loneliness and pain,
> You'd cry, "Some woman's yellow hair
> Has maddened every mother's son":
> They weighed so lightly what they gave.

> But let them be, they're dead and gone,
> They're with O'Leary in the grave.

In that stanza breathes an intense tenderness toward those generous exiles, who, though dead, have become haunting presences. It is a tenderness that almost dominates the final taunt—or plea: "But let them be. . . ." The "core" of the poem is there revealed as no rhetorical attack but a compassionate celebration of virtue. "To a Shade" carries this technique a step further. The speaker now addresses one of that "passionate serving kind" who is dead and gone. And as the poem moves to its final expression of concern for the rest and safety of that "unquiet wanderer," we again transcend the satiric taunt to contemplate a virtue that really has not died and cannot die. It lives in that still walking shade, and in the speaker's own indignant but compassionate utterance. The theme of such poems is really what Yeats called "something immortal and imperishable within himself," which the speaker finds mirrored in history.

Another poem of 1913, "To a Friend Whose Work Has Come to Nothing," brings this technique close to its tragic consummation, that joy when all falls in ruin. It is easy to distort this poem by paraphrase; to say, for example, that Yeats urges Lady Gregory to "accept the difficulty of disdaining her enemies." But the poem itself rises from consideration of the friend's defeat, her enemies' meanness, her own honorable breeding, to these final eight lines:

> Bred to a harder thing
> Than Triumph, turn away
> And like a laughing string

> Whereon mad fingers play
> Amid a place of stone,
> Be secret and exult,
> Because of all things known
> That is most difficult.

The first word, "Bred," is the poem's last clear allusion to aristocratic pride; when we reach that imperative, "Be secret and exult," it has been charged with more important meanings. For the language defines and enacts the rose blooming on the cross. The laughing string, like the poem itself, is enabled to give us its sweet music by the very insanity of the historical forces that play upon it. That place of stone is its crucifixion and its transcendence —the "flagstone under all," the "root of the world." And the final motive offered for such tragic joy is not enmity, disdain, or even pride, but the fascination of what's difficult. Shelley had said in the *Defence of Poetry* that heroes may be poetic ideals even though "remote from moral perfection," because the "vices" of a poet's contemporaries, the peculiar errors of age or class, are but "the temporary dress in which his creation must be arrayed, and which cover without concealing the eternal proportions of their beauty." Yeats was now developing a technique whereby the poem itself refines away that temporary dress and finally reveals the eternal proportions.

In their increasingly rich and energetic fusions of the temporal and the eternal, of action and contemplation, these Edwardian poems point ahead toward "Sailing to Byzantium," where the last stanza exultantly presents, in a vision of luminous form, both the transcendent desire and the actual attainment of the speaker, who sings of time in his artifice of eternity. And they point toward "Lapis Lazuli," where a similar drama is played out on the stage of universal history. Though Yeats now adds a separate contemplative section, as in "Adam's Curse," its mood is the "solar" joy of a Dionysian tragic chorus. Those Eastern sages stare upon the destruction of Apollonian heroes and of all Western civilization, and they silently proclaim their message of eternal life:

> Their eyes mid many wrinkles, their eyes,
> Their ancient, glittering eyes, are gay.

In those stony lineaments we can no longer distinguish time's ruins from eternity's mansions.

III

We may now ask what had happened, during the Edwardian period, to Yeats's early ideals of equality, charity, and peace. It is evident that in transcending history his poems also transcend the vices which belong to that realm. Their core is not anger or contempt but a kind of love, the celebration of a virtue. But my earlier remarks, like most discussions of Yeats, have too simply implied the ethics of a semi-Nietzschean heroic vitalism. We should not ignore in Yeats's work a complementary view of history and its transcendence. The poet may rise through the realm of arrogance and violence, the realm of "warring egotisms," and enter that of charity, self-judgment, and peace. These terms may be surprising, but Yeats often sanctions them, and his poetry fulfills their implications—at first hesitantly, and then with magnificence.

The early Yeats had drawn from Shelley and Blake the view that true art, created by the imagination and not by the self-deceiving will, reveals the nature of man and the cosmos. The "world as imagination sees it is the durable world"; the "laws of art" are the "hidden laws of life." Furthermore, the "sympathy with all living things, sinful and righteous alike, which the imaginative arts awaken, is that forgiveness of sins commanded by Christ." It follows that most didactic literature is not art; it is not forgiveness but accusation of sin, "not of the Father but of Satan, the accuser." True art is also symbolic, expressive, apocalyptic. False art is "mimetic, not from experience but from observation, and it is the mother of all evil, persuading us to save our bodies alive at no matter what cost of rapine and fraud." In 1901 Yeats could still say that "behind the momentary self, which acts and lives in the world, there is that which cannot be called before any mortal Judgement seat"; that great literature is therefore "the Forgiveness of Sin"; and that "when we find it becoming the Accusation of Sin, as in George Eliot, who plucks her Tito in pieces with as much assurance as if he had been clockwork, literature has begun to change into something else." [18]

When Yeats began to celebrate the temporal body, much of this view remained intact. The temporal is the vehicle of the spiritual; the poems transcend the self that acts in the world to celebrate the eternal lineaments of all selves. Furthermore, Yeats now meant by the "body" that Blakean wholeness of being which is inseparable from a joyous acceptance of life, and which is inconsistent with self-righteous or repressive moralism, political abstraction, or any hatred or violence born of a defensive incompleteness. "In a country like Ireland," he said in 1904, where abstractions "have taken the place of life, men have more hate than love, for the unhuman is nearly the same as the inhuman, but literature, which is a part of that charity that is the forgiveness of sins, will make us understand men no matter how little they conform to our expectations." [19]

However, as the speaker of Yeats's poetry committed himself increasingly to the temporal, engaging in satirical attacks and celebrating an aristocratic order that is maintained by violence, he drew upon himself a more severe refining away of dross than occurs in "September 1913" or "To a Friend Whose Work Has Come to Nothing." For Yeats could not restrict in his poetry that acute ethical sensibility evident in his analyses of Irish politics and his assessments of George Russell, John Shawe-Taylor, and John Synge. In 1909 he said that style is "self-conquest"; in 1910 he referred to "that purification from insincerity, vanity, malignity, arrogance, which is the discovery of style." And he was developing a newly purgatorial conception of the tragic character. This he saw in the "tragic ecstasy" of Synge's Deirdre: "at last when Deirdre, in the paroxysm before she took her life, touched with compassionate fingers him that had killed her lover, . . . we too were carried beyond time and persons to where passion, living through its thousand purgatorial years, as in the wink of an eye, becomes wisdom." [20] In "the twinkling of an eye, at the last trump," the corruptible puts on incorruption—and Yeats has come very close to the ethical implications of that saying. If we translate this into his own poetic world, we see that as the aristocratic and satirical poet is "carried beyond time" he must recognize in himself the voice of satanic pride and accusation. His poem must become a self-judgment.

Of course, Yeats could put this view in deceptively romantic terms. "To speak of one's emotions," he said in 1910, "without fear or moral ambition, . . . to be utterly oneself, that is all the Muses care for." But note his example: "Villon, pander, thief and man-slayer, is as immortal in their eyes, and illustrates in the cry of his ruin as great a truth as Dante in abstract ecstasy, and touches our compassion more." And he added: "All art is the disengaging of a soul from place and history, its suspension in a beautiful or terrible light to await the Judgement, though it must be, seeing that all its days were a Last Day, judged already." Blake had said that a "Last Judgment" occurs whenever "any Individual Rejects Error & Embraces Truth." Yeats saw in Synge "an unmoved mind where there is a perpetual last day, a trumpeting, and coming up to judgment." [21] And that was his own increasingly clear ideal.

Again he was really discovering the full meaning of his earlier theory. Taken in an ethical sense, his statement that the poetic genius puts on "the temporal body, which is Satan, on purpose that it might be consumed," points directly to that later poem "The Choice," which holds that the poet who chooses "perfection of the work" must "refuse / A heavenly mansion, raging in the dark." He must himself experience "the day's vanity, the night's remorse." In order to avoid the self-deceiving rhetoric of moral accusation, he must explore the fallen world in his own person and raise it, through purgatorial contemplation, to a Last Judgment. As Yeats clearly knew, Jacob Boehme had so justified the very existence of the temporal world. According to Boehme's cosmic cycle, the unmanifest Desire becomes incarnate in the egocentric variety of Nature so that it may then transform itself into a "crystalline, clear Nature" purged of self-will. And that harmony of self-realization and self-sacrifice, of variety and unity, is the goal of Yeats's own alchemical and poetic work. Then, in the phrase of an early poem, God may "burn Nature with a kiss," but without annihilation.[22]

That is why Yeats often suggested that the "artist's joy" is "of one substance with that of sanctity." Nor was he merely echoing Shelley and Blake. In 1901 he said, "there is only one perfection and only one search for perfection, and it sometimes has the form of the religious life and sometimes of the artistic life; and I do not think these lives differ in their wages, for 'The end of art is peace'. . . ." He was paraphrasing Coventry Patmore; and Patmore again is behind his distinction in 1913 between the soul revealed in art and that revealed in moral rhetoric: "A soul shaken by the spectacle of its sins, or discovered by the Divine Vision in tragic delight, must offer to the love that cannot love but to infinity a goal unique and unshared; while a soul busied with others' sins is soon melted to some shape of vulgar pride." In fact, Patmore reinforced much of Yeats's position. The peace of art, according to Patmore, is that which Aquinas called the "tranquillity of order" and considered identical with joy. It involves, "in its fullest perfection, at once the complete subdual and the glorification of the senses, and the 'ordering of all things strongly and sweetly from end to end.'" Such art, expressing a soul's unique "beauty and felicity," combines purity and passion. For "virtues are nothing but ordered passions, and vices nothing but passions in disorder."[23]

Yeats's poetry moves toward that glorification and subdual of the senses by combining in various ways the speaker's "tragic delight" and his purgatorial recognition of his own vices. As he is "carried beyond time," he orders his passions by recognizing their disorder. Sometimes this is explicit. In *Responsibilities,* after "September 1913" and "To a Friend Whose Work Has Come to Nothing," Yeats placed as a deliberate counterweight "Paudeen." There the speaker rises from his blind, stumbling indignation at stupidity and spite to the perception, born in upon him by the "luminous wind,"

> That on the lonely height where all are in God's eye,
> There cannot be, confusion of our sound forgot,
> A single soul that lacks a sweet crystalline cry.

The recognition of Boehme's "crystalline Nature" in others purifies the darkly egocentric speaker himself. And after the next satirical poem, "To a Shade," Yeats placed the wry admission—humbler even than its original prose idea—of "When Helen Lived." [24]

But Yeats soon tried to merge the active voice of social criticism with the contemplative voice of self-purgation. This occurs, still uneasily, in the poem of 1914 that closes *Responsibilities.* It begins with the illumination brought by that wind among the reeds which speaks of a transcendental realm:

> While I, from that reed-throated whisperer
> Who comes at need, although not now as once
> A clear articulation in the air,
> But inwardly, surmise companions
> Beyond the fling of the dull ass's hoof
> —Ben Jonson's phrase—and find when June is come

At Kyle-na-no under that ancient roof
A sterner conscience and a friendlier home,
I can forgive even that wrong of wrongs,
Those undreamt accidents that have made me
—Seeing that Fame has perished this long while,
Being but a part of ancient ceremony—
Notorious, till all my priceless things
Are but a post the passing dogs defile.

Amazingly enough, the syntactical heart of that *tour de force*
of invective is the statement, "I can forgive." Forgive what? Not
persons but "accidents," the impersonal process of history that
has caused his plight. The speaker accepts his lot and blames no
one for producing it, though he notes the existence of some asses
and dogs; and he honestly recognizes that his minimal forgiveness is possible only while he is supported by the surmised "companions" and by that "sterner conscience" and "friendlier home."
In other words, he defines quite exactly the proud and precarious
nature of his moral equilibrium. And we see that ethically as
well as aesthetically, the goal of the power that measures is to
transcend all measurement. For the speaker judges his limited
self in the light of an inward voice or luminous wind that he but
imperfectly incarnates.

This poem indicates one important direction in which Yeats
would soon move. He would dramatize the history of his time
in utterances that fuse proud assertion and honest admission,
social criticism and tragic purgation:

Out of Ireland have we come,
Great hatred, little room,

> Maimed us at the start.
> I carry from my mother's womb
> A fanatic heart.

He would become a scapegoat, a historical victim, taking upon himself the sins of his time—in "Nineteen Hundred and Nineteen," where he traffics in mockery, in "Meditations in Time of Civil War," where he admits the brutality of his heart, or in "Parnell's Funeral," where he cries:

> Come, fix upon me that accusing eye.
> I thirst for accusation.

If he would also write "profane" poems, the finest of them attack only a repressive and hypocritical spirituality, and they measure their profanity by a more inclusive light. There is, of course, that famous conclusion:

> Homer is my example and his unchristened heart.
> The lion and the honeycomb, what has Scripture said?
> So get you gone, Von Hügel, though with blessings on your
>   head.

Homer is *my* example: Yeats refers to the vocation of the poet. Art, he said in 1913, is "sanctity's scapegrace brother." The poet must therefore take upon himself the Satanic body, declare it, measure it, and consume it. Only so may he order "all things strongly and sweetly from end to end." As Yeats said of the Irish, "If we were . . . bitter beyond all the people of the world, we might yet lie—that too declared and measured—nearest the honeyed comb." [25] Even in "The Tower," which renders that tragic consummation when the world itself slips away in death, the speaker honestly faces all his bitterness and delirium. Not merely because it contains a testament does that poem recall Yeats's tribute to Villon, who "illustrates in the cry of his ruin as great a truth as Dante" and "touches our compassion more."

Such a poetry, which emerges in the theory and practice of Yeats's Edwardian phase, is not didactic. "The arts have nothing to give," he said, "but that joy of theirs which is the other side of sorrow, that exhausting contemplation." His art is therefore closer to the static comedy of Joyce than to the kinetic novels and dramas of Wells and Shaw. Nevertheless, Yeats could agree from a respectful distance with Shaw's dictum that "fine art is the only teacher except torture." In all great art, Yeats said, "although it does not command—indeed because it does not— may lie the roots of far-branching events. Only that which does not teach, . . . which does not persuade, . . . is irresistible." [26] That is so, he believed, because art is created not by the will, with its subtle deceptions and coercions, but by the imagination. Its power is the attraction of beauty, the splendor of truth. We should therefore not be misled by the fact that Yeats increasingly dramatized in his own person the arrogance and violence of our time. When the speaker of this poetry is carried beyond historical action into contemplation and self-judgment, he remains true to Yeats's early belief—drawn from Shelley but not merely romantic—that "the man of virtuous soul commands not nor obeys" and that "beauty . . . leads us by that love whose service is perfect freedom." [27] The end of such art is a joyous peace, not of sanctity but of tragic self-knowledge.

H. G. Wells Tries to Be a Novelist

GORDON N. RAY

My title may seem paradoxical. H. G. Wells wrote more than forty long works of fiction, and for a quarter of a century he vied with Arnold Bennett for the title of "most famous living English novelist." To the great public he was as surely a novelist as Shaw was a playwright.

Obviously, then, I employ the word "novelist" in a special sense, the high sense in which it was used by James and Conrad when they set out as conscious literary artists to make the novel the equal of the other great literary forms. Many critics today appear to assume that Wells's work has no relation to the novel so conceived, that throughout his long life he was by intent and in fact a journalist rather than an artist. Hence the astonishment professed by some reviewers of the recently published volume of James-Wells correspondence. Confronted by unmistakable evidence of fifteen years of friendly association and lively intellectual exchange between these two writers, they exclaimed: "What brought such disparate minds together at all?" [1]

I shall try to demonstrate that such an attitude towards Wells and his work can be sustained only by ignoring the most productive and interesting period of his career. Between 1895 and 1910 Wells defined for himself an ideal of the novel to which he gave embodiment in four fine books, *Love and Mr. Lewisham* (1900), *Kipps* (1905), *Tono-Bungay* (1909), and *The History of Mr. Polly* (1910). He was an acknowledged champion of serious fiction against the "novel of commerce." And he was the friend and trusted colleague of such writers as Arnold Bennett, Conrad, Stephen Crane, and George Gissing, as well as James.

For various reasons Wells afterwards turned his back on literature and "the Novel," declaring: "I am a journalist, . . . I refuse to play the 'artist.' " [2] Through a series of perverse disavowals of artistic intent, of which *Boon* and his *Experiment in Autobiography* are the most salient, he succeeded in concealing from many readers his earlier literary achievement. In this paper I propose by viewing his early work in historical perspective, unobscured by this later smoke screen, to show how Wells became "a Novelist," what he accomplished during his period of devotion to the genre, and why he eventually turned his pen to other employments.

I

It is first necessary to recapitulate what lay behind Wells when he drifted into literature in 1895. Born in 1866 into the lower-middle class, the son of a lady's maid and a shopkeeper in a small way, he grew up in the London suburb of Bromley. He received a sketchy elementary education in one of the feeble private "Academies" which still competed against the National Schools created by the Education Act of 1870. After two unhappy years as a draper's apprentice, he escaped to a position as a Grammar School teacher, from which he eventually won a scholarship to Normal School of Science in South Kensington. He made a brilliant beginning there as a pupil of Huxley, but a variety of distractions forced him once more into provincial teaching before he could take his degree.

Returning to London, he became a University Correspondence College teacher of science and a writer on scientific and educational subjects. Having made a certain reputation in these technical fields, he succeeded in gaining a precarious foothold as a literary journalist with Harry Cust's *Pall Mall Gazette* and Henley's *National Observer*. Meanwhile, he had to battle constant ill health and to survive a tangled and exhausting personal life. At a time when he knew few women, he fell in love with and married his cousin, only to find her timid nature and commonplace mind profoundly incompatible. Within two years he eloped with the brightest and liveliest of his Correspondence College students, but for some time was unable to marry her because of his wife's unwillingness to permit a divorce.

In 1895 Wells's obscure origins, his scattered and inconsecutive education, his untidy domestic arrangements, his physical weakness, and his long history of false starts in life did not seem to hold much promise for the future. But in fact he was prepared, as was no gently born and reared Oxford or Cambridge "First," to understand his society and his age. The old order was breaking up, and he was the representative figure of the new, "an individual becoming the conscious Common Man of his time and culture." [3] And, of course, he was clearly a genius.

II

Wells saw that the big opportunities for the writer of his time were in fiction. But he was conscious of an "exceptional ignorance of the contemporary world," and he accordingly set about "exploring the possibilities of fantasy." "That is the proper game for the young man," he later remarked, "particularly for the young man without a natural social setting of his own." [4] Between 1895 and 1897 *The Time Machine, The Island of Dr. Moreau,* and *The Invisible Man* began the long series of books which were to make him the unrivaled master of what has come to be called "science fiction."

Meanwhile, Wells was also formulating his conception of what the novel proper should be and preparing to make his mark as well in this more demanding field. He was assisted in this effort, it might almost be said that he was impelled to it, through his employment by Frank Harris as a contributor to the *Saturday Review.* At first his writing and reviewing were confined to scientific and educational topics, but in time he became the *Saturday*'s chief reviewer of fiction. The resulting series of articles in which he surveyed contemporary fiction between 1895 and 1897 bears comparison with Shaw's more extensive series on the contemporary stage in the same magazine. Their importance and indeed in most instances their very existence have not previously been recognized, because all but a few are unsigned. Only through a close study of the files of the *Saturday Review,* guided by clues in the Wells papers at the University of Illinois, has it been possible to establish with some certainty the canon of his contributions.[5]

Essential to Wells's view of the fiction of his day was his estimate of the public which read it. "The coming to reading age in 1886–1888 of multitudes of boys and girls [educated in the schools created by the act of 1870] . . . changed the conditions of journalism and literature in much the same way as the French Rev-

olution changed the conditions of political thought and action."
The new male readers degraded journalism, the new female
readers debased fiction. Thus was to be explained "the comparative popularity to-day of scores of books whose relation to
life is of the slightest, and whose connexion with art is purely
accidental. It is scarcely too much to say that every writer of our
time who can be called popular owes three-quarters of his or her
fame to the girls who have been taught in Board schools." [6]

Consequently Wells held that "the public criticism of fiction, as
distinguished from the reviewing of books for purposes of advertisement, should be primarily the court of appeal from the popular judgment. Therein the conscientious writer should find the
consolation for his hard-won failure, and the successful impostor
the end of his complacency. And the latter is, perhaps, the more
important function of the two. To permit Mr. Hall Caine to
pass off his violent posings, Mr. Hocking his pious novelettes, and
Mr. Ian Maclaren his blend of Thrums and street-preaching, as
reputable writing, or to allow Miss Marie Corelli to assume the
place the vulgar Lady assigns her without protest, is to do the
art of fiction—the most vital and typical art of this country and
period—a serious disservice. The standard of criticism must be
consistently high, its methods severe." [7]

Following these precepts faithfully, Wells made himself a
militant champion of the good against the bad in fiction. Not
limiting himself to the portentous sensation novels of Hall Caine
and Marie Corelli and the twaddling tales which Hocking and
the "Whimpering Scotch humourists" wrote for the Sunday
public, he extended his attack to nearly every other species of
bad fiction that flourished at the time. He was particularly

severe on the most prosperous and prestigious fictional genre of them all, the romance, whether it was the traditional "Wardour Street" species of Sir Walter Besant, the "blood-and-thunder" variety practiced by Rider Haggard, or the "chromatic story-telling" favored by imitators of Stevenson and Stanley Weyman. "The romance form prohibits anything but the superficialities of self-expression," Wells contended; "and sustained humour, subtle characterization, are impossible." He could bring himself to praise *Weir of Hermiston* only by describing its author as "not so much a romancer as a novelist entangled in the puerilities of romance," [8] and he consistently underestimated even such superior romances of the period as *The Prisoner of Zenda, The Three Impostors,* and *The Splendid Spur.* Indeed, when Wells later wished to suggest the profound intellectual poverty of Mr. Stanley, Ann Veronica's father, he presented him as a man who "read but little, and that chiefly healthy light fiction with chromatic titles, 'The Red Sword,' 'The Black Helmet,' 'The Purple Robe,' also in order 'to distract his mind.'" [9]

Wells's procedure in his reviews was original (for his time) and effective. Contemporary criticism had formed "the academic habit of criticizing deductively from admitted classics," [10] he held, and "so the dead hand of an accomplished literature oppresses us." He asked that the critic instead "be able to appreciate essentials, to understand the bearing of structural expedients upon design, to get at an author through his workmanship, to analyse a work as though it stood alone in the world." [11]

Wells's analysis took the form of minute dissection of the style, characters, and incidents of the book under discussion. Quoting and summarizing freely, he was able by means of his ironical and sometimes hilarious commentary to convict each popular favorite from his own words through accumulated instances of inconsistency, exaggeration, and bathos. Much space would be required to do justice to any of these performances, and I must pass over even his massacre of the "kail-yard school" in a review of Ian Maclaren's *A Doctor of the Old School* entitled "The Simple Art of Popular Pathos," [12] and his triumphant disposal of *The Monk of Fife*—the lone romance by Andrew Lang, erudite critical high-priest of the genre—as an example of "not so much boyishness proper as prize-boyishness." [13] His farewell to *Joan Haste* may stand as a sample of the tone of these reviews: "It is indeed a melancholy book, full of forcible foolishness, a jerry-built story with a stucco style, and it fully justifies Mr. Haggard's position beside Messrs. Hall Caine and Crockett as one of the most popular writers of our time." [14]

III

If Wells was contemptuous of the popular favorites of his day, he was profoundly respectful when he wrote of the novelists whom he admired: Stephen Crane, Conrad, Gissing, Hardy, Kipling, Meredith, George Moore, and Turgenev. He took very seriously indeed his task of providing "consolation" to the conscientious novelist for his "hard-won failure," and in the process he worked out the formula that was to guide his own efforts in fiction. This was natural enough, since he regarded the writer of great fiction—Sterne, Balzac, Dickens, and Thackeray in the past, and the writers already listed in the present—as the practitioner of a difficult and demanding calling in which success was impossible without maturity and wisdom. "To see life clearly and whole," he wrote, "to see and represent it with absolute self-detachment, with absolute justice, above all with evenly balanced sympathy, is an ambition permitted only to a man full-grown." [15]

The keystone of Wells's conception of fiction was realism. Even in his scientific narratives, he was showing himself to be, as Conrad told him in 1898, the "Realist of the Fantastic." "What impresses me," Conrad continued, "is to see how you contrive to give over humanity into the clutches of the Impossible and yet manage to keep it down (or up) to its flesh, blood, sorrow, folly." [16] Everywhere in his reviews Wells urges that the novelist should strive to convey "the precise effect of things as they actually seem to him." [17] Only by thus aiming at truthful rendering through accurate observation could he hope to attain to the indispensable element of great fiction, individual character fully realized. So Wells praises Henryk Sienkiewicz for being "among the chosen few who can see frankly, who are able to get outside the conventional puppets of fiction and give us fresh human beings for our thought and sympathy. His people are individualized wonderfully, and alive to their very finger tips. . . . One reads [*Children of the Soil*], just as one reads Balzac or Thackeray, in order to get first this light and then that on some wonderfully invented personage." [18]

But Wells asked for more than truthful observation precisely rendered, for more than individual characters fully realized. His reading of Dickens had made him aware of a "new structural conception" in that author's later novels: "the grouping of characters and incidents, no longer about a lost will, a hidden murder, or a mislaid child, but about some social influence or some far-reaching movement of humanity." He found Balzac and Zola also "displaying a group of typical individuals at the point of action of some great social force, the social force in question and not the 'hero' and 'heroine' being the real operative interest of the story." [19]

He discovered the supreme example of this kind of novel, which seemed to him "the highest form of literary art," when Constance Garnett's translation of Turgenev's *Fathers and Children* came his way for review. Wells was struck by the "extraordinary way in which [Turgenev] can make his characters typical, while at the same time retaining their individuality. . . . Turgénev people are not avatars of theories nor tendencies. They are living, breathing individuals, but individuals living under the full stress of this great social force or that. . . . We have the characters carried, not upon the tides of a man's development, but upon the secular advance in opinion which maintains a perpetual conflict between young and old. 'Bazarov,' written five-and-twenty years ago, is still typically modern—earnest to get behind sentimentality, idealism, to go hand in hand with truth. He is, says Mr. Edward Garnett, in italics, *'the bare mind of Science first applied to Politics';* and that is admirably the essence of the matter. And yet he is human, perfectly human; and therein is the wonder of Turgénev's art." [20]

It became habitual for Wells to look in the authors whom he reviewed for evidences of "an acute sense of causation," of implication, of the way the world is moving.[21] One of his major reasons for regarding *Jude the Obscure* as a masterpiece was that Hardy's protagonist spoke with "the voice of the educated proletarian, speaking more distinctly than it has ever spoken before in English literature. The man is, indeed, at once an individual and a type." [22] Again, we find him impelled to record the following reservation concerning Arthur Morrison's *A Child of the Jago,* a novel which he admired for its faithful realism and its narrative art: "He sees the Jago, is profoundly impressed by the appearance of the Jago, renders its appearance with extraordinary skill. But the origin of the Jago, the place of the Jago in the general scheme of things, the trend of change in it, its probable destiny—such matters are not in his mind." [23]

Wells was fully alert to the dangers inherent in this conception of fiction. Again and again he warned of the narrow margin separating art from propaganda. His most trenchant statement on this topic occurs in a review of Grant Allen's *The British Barbarians:* "The sooner Mr. Allen realizes that he cannot adopt an art-form and make it subservient to the purposes of the pamphleteer, the better for humanity and for his own reputation as a thinker and a man of letters. Far be it from us to curb Mr. Allen's desire to reform his generation. Let him preach to it from his hill-top till he mends it or it ends him, but let him call his sermon a sermon and be content. But the philosopher who masquerades as a novelist, violating the conditions of art that his gospel may win notoriety, discredits both himself and his message, and the result is neither philosophy nor fiction." [24]

His reading of Gissing enabled Wells to formulate another element in his conception of what the novel should be. Confronted by Gissing's "grey world of conscientious veracity," he inquired: "Is this harsh greyness really representative of life, even the life of the lower middle class who work for wages and are seedily respectable all their days? . . . There are happy omnibus conductors, clerks delighted with their lot, workgirls having the best of times, cheerful cripples, and suicidal dukes. The true Realism, we hold, looks both on the happy and on the unhappy, interweaves some flash of joy or humour into its gloomiest tragedy. Weighed by that standard, Mr. Gissing falls short. He is like Gilbert's Elderly Naval Man, 'he never larks nor plays.' . . . The fixed idea of the dismalness of middle-class life is not only the key-note of [*Eve's Ransom*], but of all his books. That evil shadow lies upon all his work; it reduces it from the level of a faithful presentation of life to *genre*. It is the *genre* of nervous exhaustion." Wells demanded, to the contrary, that the novel should be "exhilarating." [25]

Hence we find him deploring "the 'colourless' theory" of fiction. No doubt it was responsible for significant work, not only in Gissing's books, but also in those of George Moore and Stephen Crane. Yet it entailed heavy sacrifices. "Let your characters tell their own story, make no comment, write a novel as you would a play. So we are robbed of the personality of the author, in order that we may get an enhanced impression of reality." For himself Wells rejected this doctrine of rigorous suppression. He was loyal instead to the digression, to the ironical aside, in fact to all the traditional freedoms of the English novel from Sterne to Thackeray.[26] Only so could the temperament of the author, expressed through his living voice, provide the life-enhancing exhilaration that Wells regarded as a necessary part of the novel.

Wells was much less demanding with regard to narrative form. He admired *Jude the Obscure* for its "steady unfaltering progression towards one great and simple effect," [27] but he was equally happy with the multiple plots of Balzac and the great Victorians. He asked merely that "a sense of close sequence" should be operative in the novelist's mind. Only then could there emerge "one of those rare and satisfactory novels in which almost every sentence has its share in the entire design." [28]

Other points that Wells emphasized were attention to "the art of dialogue," to ensure that conversational exchanges were authentic, economical, and telling; and dramatic visual presentation. Here he confessed an individual idiosyncrasy. "All that I remember most clearly is remembered as visual images," he wrote, "—even abstract matters are remembered as symbolical diagrams. When I read such a visualizing writer as Stevenson I really see quite vividly a succession of pictures, some of extraordinary persistence; the flaring candles in the 'Master of Ballantrae' is the one thing I am absolutely sure I shall never forget of all that astonishing book." [29]

It was on this latter account that he both admired and reproved Conrad for *An Outcast of the Islands*. He thought the book "a masterpiece, . . . true, powerful, and abundantly humorous." But Conrad's visual splendor was obscured by his style. "Mr. Conrad is wordy; his story is not so much told as seen intermittently through a haze of sentences. His style is like river-mist; for a space things are seen clearly, and then comes a great grey bank of printed matter, page on page, creeping round the reader, swallowing him up. You stumble, you protest, you blunder on, for the drama you saw so cursorily has hold of you; you cannot escape until you have seen it out. You read fast, you run and jump, only to bring yourself to the knees in . . . mud. Then suddenly things loom up again, and in a moment become real, intense, swift." [30] Likewise Wells's reservations at this period regarding Henry James's work were occasioned by the latter's "ground-glass style." "By close application you can just discern through it, men and women as trees walking," Wells wrote. "Reading 'The Coxon Fund,'" he continued, "is like walking about the city on Sunday in a dense fog. Rare characters loom upon one dimly and pass, muttering incoherent nothings; vague action goes on in the penumbra; Saltram, the principal person in the drama, is especially elusive. You want to get close to him, to look him in the face; you want to say to him, 'Mr. Caliph, I believe?' and you never get the chance." [31]

The conception of the novel which Wells evolved for himself through his *Saturday* reviewing was solid and creditable, but with the important exception of his insistence on representing great social issues through individual histories, thoroughly traditional. Since he took the parlous state of popular fiction as his starting point, it was perhaps inevitable that he should not attempt to go beyond certain broad discriminations suggested by "the strong antipathy of good to bad," that he should reproach James for his "singular distaste for the obvious." [32] Certainly to turn from these reviews to Conrad's preface to *The Nigger of the Narcissus* or to James's introductions to the New York edition of his *Novels and Tales* is to enter a different universe of discourse. Most of the points which Wells makes are taken for granted, with only an offhand reference to the "unofficial sentimentalism" of popular fiction,[33] as Conrad and James seek to discriminate between the good and the best.

IV

Such was the conception of the novel which Wells worked out for himself through his *Saturday* reviewing. His success in achieving what was to be the unique feature of his work, the relating of individual histories representative of larger social forces, clearly depended, as he put it, on his ability "to study and state for my own satisfaction the social process in which we swim as fish swim in a flood of water." [34]

He had begun to grope towards such a perspective while still a frustrated and rebellious draper's apprentice. So we find him writing to his no doubt horrified mother in 1883 of "the hideous framework required by the usages of a corrupt and degenerate society." [35] During the years that followed at the Normal School of Science he quickly became a "Socialist in the Resentful Phase." Listening to speeches by Morris and Shaw, and reading Edward Bellamy and Henry George,[36] he and his friends came gradually to realize that "Something—none of us knew how to define it but we called it generally the Capitalist System—a complex of traditional usage, uncontrolled acquisitive energy and perverted opportunities, was wasting life for us." [37]

As the century turned, Wells passed from a negative to a positive socialism. He became convinced not only that the existing framework of society should be destroyed, but also that given a modicum of intelligence and good-will, it could readily be replaced with a reasonable and coherent substitute. So he wrote a series of sociological works, of which *Anticipations* (1901), *Mankind in the Making* (1903), and *A Modern Utopia* (1905) were the most prominent, criticizing the old order and proposing a new. Yet at this period he regarded these books as important to him above all for what they contributed towards his work as a novelist. "They have, I think, made a sort of view-platform of the world for me," he wrote in 1908. "If I was to become a novelist of contemporary life, that was what I had to do. There was no ready-made standing ground for me, the beliefs and assumptions of our fathers have decayed, become unsafe or altogether broken down. I had to define what I stood upon or write of life in a disconnected and inconsistent way. Now it seems to me I may hope to get on to the work that has always attracted me most and render some aspects of this great spectacle of life and feeling in which I find myself in terms of individual experience and character." [38] Thus it was that Wells, starting from an "exceptional ignorance of the contemporary world," gained the intellectual understanding of it that he needed as a frame for his fiction.

Equally important was the development of his emotional attitude towards his world, since here lies the clue to the human meaning of his novels. Between 1893 and 1896, as he established a place for himself in the literary world, his annual income mounted from less than £400 to more than £1,000.[39] He emerged once for all from the lower middle class into which he was born and in which he had spent his early life. In "Excelsior," the most personal of his articles for the *Saturday Review,* he describes what this experience meant to him.

Among his new associates such an individual, Wells discovered, "is an intruder, and largely inexplicable. . . . He knows . . . the legend of the Bounder, knows that these people credit all men who rise from his class with an aggressive ostentation, with hair-oil and at least one massive gold chain, if not two, besides a complete inversion of the horrid aspirate. He imagines that people expect breaches of their particular laws, and he knows, too, that there is some ground for that expectation. He blunders at times from sheer watchfulness." Moreover, he has become equally ill at ease in the class from which he came. "That friend, that dear friend, who is the salt of life, with whom he may let his mind run free, whose prejudices are the same, whose habits coincide," remarks, "You're getting such a Swell now, you know," and a gulf yawns. Even worse troubles beset him if he has married "someone down below there, . . . [who] cannot keep pace with him." "That is the disillusionment of the successful proletarian." And so Wells concludes: "Better a little grocery, a life of sordid anxiety, love, and a tumult of children, than this Dead Sea fruit of success." [40]

It will be noted that Wells remains loyal to the values of the lower middle class, the submerged group out of which he has risen. He said good-bye to the Kipps, the Mr. Polly, even the Mr. Lewisham in himself. He saw clearly that these were "personalities thwarted and crippled by the defects of our contemporary life." [41] He knew how completely they reflected the "perplexity, frustration, humiliation, and waste of energy [that] are the common lot of human beings in a phase of blindly changing conditions." [42] Yet whatever his intelligence told him about them, in his heart he went on regarding them as the salt of the earth.

Similarly Wells hated the upper class, the late Victorian "Establishment," which kept the lower middle class in its "place." And he felt profound contempt for the great intervening middle class which took its lead in manners and opinion from this Establishment. He would thoroughly have endorsed a classic sentence by Shaw in the last paragraph of the first chapter of *Fabian Essays in Socialism:* "since we were taught to revere proprietary respectability in our unfortunate childhood, and since we found our childish hearts so hard and unregenerate that they secretly hated and rebelled against respectability in spite of that teaching, it is impossible to express the relief with which we discover that our hearts were all along right, and that the current respectability of to-day is nothing but a huge inversion of righteous and scientific social order weltering in dishonesty, uselessness, selfishness, wanton misery, and idiotic waste of magnificent opportunities for noble and happy living." [43]

By establishing this intellectual perspective, by defining these emotional allegiances, Wells discovered that he had after all that "natural social setting of his own" which he regarded as a necessity for fiction. Like young Ponderevo in *Tono-Bungay,* he could look back at his youth, now placed and clarified by long and thoughtful consideration, "as dispassionately as one looks at a picture—at some wonderful, perfect sort of picture that is inexhaustible." [44] This reservoir of vital memories was to give him the starting point for each of his four notable novels.

v

Late in 1896 Wells set to work on his first novel along the lines that he had laid down for himself in his *Saturday* reviewing. He had previously written two narratives of middle length, *The Wonderful Visit* (1895) and *The Wheels of Chance* (1896), that are predominantly realistic pictures of contemporary life, but light and unsubstantial. *Love and Mr. Lewisham* was to be the real thing.[45] It was not finished until 1900. Meanwhile, in 1898 he had begun *Kipps,* which was completed in 1905. *Tono-Bungay* occupied him intermittently between 1905 and 1908. Only *The*

History of Mr. Polly (1910) was written consecutively in a relatively brief period.

In each of the three earlier novels Wells began, broke off, and returned to his task many times. In part this was due to his method of composition. His stories typically went through a series of drafts, growing by accretion along the way; and he often saw fit to leave a prolonged interval of time between one draft and the next. But there were other reasons why it took him twelve years to write *Love and Mr. Lewisham, Kipps,* and *Tono-Bungay.*

Henley had warned Wells in 1895: "For Heaven's sake take care of yourself. You have a unique talent; and—you've published three books, at least, within the year, & are up to the elbows in a fourth. It is magnificent, of course; but it can't be literature." [46] Wells turned a deaf ear to this caution. "I was a journalist living from hand to mouth," he later explained to a correspondent, "& I thought it wiser to turn out a succession of striking if rather unfinished books & so escape from journalism than to let myself be forgotten again while I elaborated a masterpiece saving my limitations." [47] By the time success and recognition came his way, he was caught in this pattern of hurried overproduction and could not change it.

The initiation of *Love and Mr. Lewisham* in 1896 was his gesture towards a masterpiece, saving his limitations, his effort to raise himself in the literary hierarchy so that he might cease to be "a sort of literary page in the train of Caine Zangwill & so forth." [48] He was prepared to take infinite pains with the novel, to put it in a quite different category from the rest of his work, but he had little faith in its marketability with a public which looked to him for very different things. *"Love and Mr. Lewisham* is a drug,"* he told his agent Pinker in 1898. "It's not like Jacobs & it's not like Jules Verne, & I must be dead & stinking according to the rules before anyone will find any merit in its being like me." [49] Even when it was about to appear in 1900 he complained to Bennett: "Why the Hell have you joined the conspiracy to restrain me to one particular type of story? I want to write novels & before God I *will* write novels." [50]

When *Love and Mr. Lewisham* in fact attracted no particular attention, there was small incentive for Wells to press on with *Kipps.* "I am doomed to write 'scientific' romances & short stories for you creatures of the mob," he told Bennett, "and my novels must be my private dissipation." [51] But he persisted, and with *Kipps* in 1905 he did hit "the big public," though not "the Corellian public," at last. He was now fully established as a novelist; but by this time the dispersion of his literary energies among a variety of projects had become a habit which he could not change, and the writing of *Tono-Bungay* required three years. Its appearance left him in a mood of supreme confidence. *"My* novel," he wrote in the copy presented to Bennett,[52] who had recently sent him *The Old Wives' Tale.* And in this mood of euphoria he conceived and rapidly completed *The History of Mr. Polly.*

This then is the external history of Wells's four true novels. He lavished immense pains upon them. "So far as labour and thought count in these things," he wrote of *Love and Mr. Lewisham,* "writing it was an altogether more serious undertaking than anything I have ever done before." [53] This applies as well to the books that followed. But nevertheless a penalty had to be paid for the discontinuities in their composition, and except for *The*

History of Mr. Polly it cannot be claimed that they are perfectly harmonious and consistent works of art.

VI

Wells found the materials for *Love and Mr. Lewisham* in the decade (1883–93) that spanned his service as an assistant master at Midhurst Grammar School, his years as a student at the Normal School of Science, and his courtship of, marriage to, and eventual parting from his cousin Isabel. Lewisham's experiences follow those of Wells in broad outline, yet the changes are so numerous and important that the book is in no sense autobiography. Lewisham is in most respects very like what Wells had been at twenty. He possesses Wells's ambition, but he is deprived of Wells's genius and drive, and thus becomes a more typical figure through whose career the larger social forces of the time may be illustrated. Ethel, the girl with whom he falls in love, contains many reminiscences of Isabel. Otherwise Wells was scrupulous in avoiding portraits of actual persons.[54]

Love and Mr. Lewisham is the most carefully constructed and shapely of Wells's novels. It is the one book, indeed, that he wrote to a scenario, and enough survives of the manuscript[55] to show how carefully he pruned his narrative by dropping all episodes and characters not essential to the economical development of the story. Apart from the two principals, indeed, only three characters—Miss Heydinger, Chaffery, and Mme Gadow—are presented with any fullness.

The novel is a classic example of the hourglass pattern. In chapter one we meet Lewisham in his lodgings near the school where he is an assistant master. On the wall hangs a "Schema" of the events which are to lead him to "Greatness." "In this scheme, 1892 was indicated as the year in which Mr. Lewisham proposed to take his B.A. degree at the London University with 'hons. in all subjects,' and 1895 as the date of his 'gold medal.' Subsequently there were to be 'pamphlets in the Liberal interest,' and such-like things duly dated." Elsewhere there dangles a "Time-Table" which enjoins Mr. Lewisham to rise at five, pursue French until eight, and then "varies its injunctions for the rest of the twenty-four hours according to the day of the week." [56]

Ethel appears, and during Lewisham's flirtation with her, the Schema is forgotten. But they are quickly separated, and for three years Lewisham returns to the pursuit of his ambitions. Then they meet again, under the most unpropitious circumstances. Lewisham is a promising scholarship student at South Kensington. She is assisting her stepfather Chaffery in imposing his deceptions upon devotees of spiritualism. Lewisham knows that he should avoid her, but he cannot. When he finally seeks her out, Wells writes, "they stood face to face at the cardinal point of their lives." [57] The balance in Lewisham's mind has swung from his career to love. The difficulties of courtship make it impossible for him to maintain his work at scholarship level. Any remaining chance of retrieving his position is lost when he marries Ethel and has to seek out an inferior teaching position to support her and, as it shortly develops, her mother.

In the final chapter, entitled "The Crowning Victory," Wells offers his interpretation of this story. We see the Lewishams a year or two later, when their first child is expected. Encountering by chance his forgotten Schema, he reflects:

"Yes it was vanity, . . . A boy's vanity. For me—anyhow.
. . . We must perish in the wilderness—Some day. Some-
when. But not for us. . . . Come to think, it is all the Child.
The future is the Child. . . . And yet—it is almost as if
Life had played me a trick—promised so much—given so
little! . . ."

His eyes came back to the Schema. . . . The vision of that
arranged Career, that ordered sequence of work and suc-
cesses, distinctions and yet further distinctions, rose brightly
from the symbol. Then he compressed his lips and tore the
yellow sheet in half. . . .

"It is the end of adolescence," he said; "the end of empty
dreams. . . ."

He became very still, his hands resting on the table, his eyes
staring out of the blue oblong of the window. The dwindling
light gathered itself together and became a star.[58]

Thus does Wells reiterate the conclusion of "Excelsior": "Better
. . . a life of sordid anxiety, love, and a tumult of children, than
this Dead Sea fruit of success."

Because of the novel's narrow focus, the social frame in which
Lewisham works out his destiny is suggested in occasional
asides [59] rather than presented. Yet chapter 25, in which he first
seeks employment in London by going the round of the teachers'
agencies, only to discover how limited is his marketability and
what compromises with principle he must make to get any job
at all, tells much by implication. The state of English secondary
education generally can be deduced with some precision from this

chapter, and it places Lewisham for the reader to see how he fits into this system.

Finally there is the justification offered by Ethel's stepfather, Chaffery, when Lewisham taxes him with cheating at the séances which he arranges for wealthy gulls:

> "I don't think you fully appreciate the importance of Illusion in life, the Essential Nature of Lies and Deception of the body politic. . . . Now I am prepared to maintain . . . that Honesty is essentially an anarchistic and disintegrating force in society, that communities are held together and the progress of civilisation made possible only by vigorous and sometimes even violent Lying; that the Social Contract is nothing more nor less than a vast conspiracy of human beings to lie to and humbug themselves and one another for the general Good. Lies are the mortar that bind the savage individual man into the social masonry. . . . Most respectable positions in the world are tainted with the fraud of our social conditions. If they were not tainted with fraud they would not be respectable. . . . Since all ways of life are tainted with fraud, since to live and speak the truth is beyond human strength and courage—as one finds it—is it not better for a man that he engage in some straight-forward comparatively harmless cheating, than if he risk his mental integrity in some ambiguous position and fall at last into deception and self-righteousness?" [60]

Wells preserved the good-will of conventional readers by attributing these outrageous opinions to an admitted scoundrel with a taste for fantastic paradox. But the more penetrating contemporary critics (Bennett among them) were not deceived. They recognized that Chaffery's highly subversive view of society was Wells's own, that his role in the novel was in fact very like that of the *raisonneur* in the well-made play of the period. Certainly, if Chaffery's confession of faith is taken into account, as Lewisham "fades from us into a mist of undistinguishable lives," [61] Wells has not failed to embody in his history the social forces that controlled the destiny of the lower middle class in late Victorian England.

Within its conventions the realism of *Love and Mr. Lewisham* is absolute. The reader never thinks of questioning the fidelity with which Wells renders this world which he knows so intimately. With respect to persuasiveness of depiction, for example, his picture of student life in South Kensington sustains comparison with Joyce's picture of student life in Dublin in *A Portrait of the Artist as a Young Man*. The reader's reservation is apt to be that Wells's passion for authenticity leaves the novel somewhat subdued and underdeveloped. Except for the occasional chapters devoted to Chaffery and his adventures in spiritualism,[62] the startling eccentrics and the broad comedy that Dickens had taught Wells to see in life are missing.

Yet the total effect of the book is anything but depressing. Its pages are lit up by wit, as when Wells describes the English socialists of the 1880s, "going about the walls of the Social Jericho, blowing their own trumpets," or tells his readers: "Monday dawned coldly and clearly—a Herbert Spencer of a day." A quiet humor lurks in many scenes, as in Wells's account of the youthful Lewisham's conversion to socialism:

So he went out and (historical moment) bought that red tie.

"Blood colour, please," said Lewisham meekly to the young lady at the counter.

"*What* colour?" said the young lady at the counter, sharply.

"A bright scarlet, please," said Lewisham, blushing.

And though his novel, like *Born in Exile* and *Jude the Obscure,* deals with the iron constraint imposed by the late Victorian social order on native ability unsupported by birth and acceptable training, *Love and Mr. Lewisham* has none of the painfulness of those two books. Wells shows the boredom, the exasperation, and the fear in the hampered lives he is describing, but he is also tenderly aware of the possibilities of happiness and self-realization which they offer. He assures the reader: "There was more than a touch of magnificence, you perceive, about this affair." [63]

In writing *Love and Mr. Lewisham* Wells sought to produce a conscious "work of art, . . . very clear, simple, graceful, and human," [64] and he attained his goal. But it remains a novel of limited aims, occupying in Wells's work much the same place that *The Nigger of the "Narcissus"* does in Conrad's or *Anna of the Five Towns* in Bennett's. It is an admirable achievement which commands liking and respect; yet even contemporary readers were not dazzled and overwhelmed by it, as they were by *Kipps* and *Tono-Bungay.*

VII

Impatient with the restraints that the careful organization of *Love and Mr. Lewisham* had imposed upon him, restraints which led him to say that ever afterwards "the Laocoön reminded him of nothing so much as a novelist struggling with a scenario," [65] Wells determined to make *Kipps* a "great novel on the Dickens plan," [66] in which he would write as the spirit moved him. For a time he had in mind a vast trilogy tracing a moderate fortune as it passed through several hands. In the first part, which he called "The Wealth of Mr. Waddy," he told of the declining years of the eccentric and irascible Waddy, with whom the fortune originated. In the second part, the only portion of the novel to be published, this money transforms the life of Kipps. The third part, which remained unwritten, was to have related what use young Mr. Walsingham made of the fortune "as a fugitive in France," after embezzling it from Kipps. In 1925 when Wells wrote his introduction to *Kipps* for the Atlantic Edition, he thought that "The Wealth of Mr. Waddy" had been "destroyed." [67] The manuscript of "those abandoned chapters" in fact survives at the University of Illinois, though unfortunately not in anything like final form. For our immediate purposes, however, it is enough to know that *Kipps* is a fragment of a colossal whole, written with a sense of freedom to improvise, to digress, to amplify, which makes it a quite different kind of novel from *Love and Mr. Lewisham*.

For the first book of *Kipps* Wells went further back into his past than he had in his earlier novel, to his childhood years at Bromley and particularly to his "two years of servitude" as an apprentice in the Southsea Drapery Emporium (1881–83), which, he said in his old age, had been his only period of real unhappiness.[68] The most oppressive aspect of these years had been the seeming impossibility of escape, the feeling that this mechanical drudgery and maddening servility would stretch out indefinitely. In writing *Kipps* Wells asked himself: if I had been an ordinary fellow who had to serve the full seven years of apprenticeship, instead of an intellectual phenomenon who broke loose through sheer will power after two, what then might my character and life have been?

The remainder of the novel, the much larger portion that follows Kipps's inheritance of Mr. Waddy's fortune, derives from the more recent experiences touched upon in "Excelsior." As early as 1895 in a *Saturday* review Wells had declared his conviction that "there is no more elaborately built structure of mental artificialities than our current middle-class ideas and ways of life." [69] But this cool appraisal of society's worth did not save him from a decade of painful adjustments as he took his place in it. "We English . . . ," he wrote in a heartfelt passage, "live in a strange atmosphere of neglected great issues, of insistent, triumphant, petty things; we are given up to the fine littlenesses of intercourse; table manners and small correctitudes are the substance of our lives. . . . The mists of noble emotion swirl and pass, and there you are divorced from all your deities and grazing in the meadows under the Argus eyes of the social system, the innumerable mean judgments you feel raining upon you, upon your clothes and bearing, upon your pretensions and movements." [70]

This account of the origins of *Kipps* in Wells's life explains why it is a "fighting" book,[71] in which Wells's jaundiced view of English life finds far fuller and more effective expression than it had in *Love and Mr. Lewisham*. He is still sufficiently cautious, however, to entrust the task of tying together the threads of his indictment to a spokesman who need not be taken seriously by the conventional reader. This time it is Masterman, a dying socialist intellectual, who voices Wells's opinions, albeit in exaggerated form, in a tirade against the society which has beaten him. "The world is out of joint," Masterman contends, "and there isn't a soul alive who isn't half waste or more." "This society we live in is ill. It's a fractious, feverish invalid, gouty, greedy and ill nourished." "Monotony and toil and contempt and dishonour" make up the lot of the poor. And the well-to-do are no better off. "Money, like everything else, is a deception and a disappointment. . . . As for happiness, you want a world in order before money or property, or any of those things have any real value." [72]

The truth of these charges with regard to the lower classes is abundantly demonstrated in the vivid chapters devoted to Kipps's apprentice life in the Folkestone Drapery Bazaar. The dilemma of Kipps and his fellows—worse than that of manual workers because of "the cheapness of the genteeler sorts of labour"—is summed up by the spirited Minton, who eventually goes off to be a soldier: "I tell you we're in a blessed drainpipe, and we've got to crawl along it till we die." Kipps perceives dimly "how the great stupid machine of retail trade had caught his life into its wheels, a vast irresistible force which he had neither strength of will nor knowledge to escape. . . . And there was a terrible something called the 'swap,' or 'the key of the street,' and 'crib hunting,' of which the talk was scanty but sufficient. Night after night he would resolve to enlist, to run away to sea, to set fire to the warehouse, or drown himself; and morning after morning he rose up and hurried downstairs in fear of a sixpenny fine." [73]

Nor does Kipps's escape from poverty to opulence mend matters. While he was submerged in the lower middle class there had been drilled into him a nervous horror of being thought "low." Thus conditioned, he takes it for granted that having money imposes an obligation to strive conscientiously for refinement. He forms an alliance with Mr. Chester Coote, "a conscious gentleman, equally aware of society and the serious side of life," who in his eyes is "the type of the hidden thing called culture." Under Coote's tutelage he seeks to master the code and manners of good society. He has no talent for this sort of assimilation, however, and he soon finds himself in a state of constant embarrassment in comparison with which his former life seems in retrospect almost easy. Even more painful to him are his attempts to observe Coote's admonition that "a leading solicitude of the true gentleman is to detect clearly those 'beneath' him, and to behave towards them in a proper spirit." Kipps makes an ineffective snob, but even so he has to approach himself with "murdered Friendships" which cause him profound remorse.[74]

Kipps's adventure in gentlemanliness culminates in his determination to embark upon "the high enterprise of marrying above his breeding."[75] He chooses, or more correctly he is chosen by, a Miss Walsingham, whose art class he had attended while still a draper's apprentice. In his new position even the most trivial social occasion becomes an unbearable trial. At last exhausted nature can bear no more, and he elopes with his boyhood sweetheart, Ann, whom he has encountered as a housemaid in one of the houses where he visits. It appears at first that their marriage is doomed to failure because Kipps is still infected with dim notions of refinement and snobbery which Ann cannot share. The abrupt loss of most of his fortune cures him of this folly. And we leave him, vague and inarticulate to the last but wiser about the things that matter, established comfortably with Ann in a little bookshop. Once more, it will be observed, Wells is faithful to the conclusion of "Excelsior."

Wells's chief means of interpreting his story is the bright, intelligent, ironic voice in which he tells it. He stands beside Kipps, displaying him with affection and compassion; and as the reader listens to his account of the impressions experienced by this naïve and confused but honest and decent young man, the unfairness and absurdity of the social order of which he is a part is brought home irresistibly. No wonder, then, that Henry James thought *Kipps* a "born gem," and praised Wells for having written "the first intelligently and consistently ironic or satiric novel." [76] Only once does Wells find it necessary to step to the center of the stage with a summary of his meaning:

> The stupid little tragedies of these clipped and limited lives!
>
> As I think of them lying unhappily there in the darkness, my vision pierces the night. See what I can see! Above them, brooding over them, I tell you there is a monster, a lumpish monster, like some great clumsy griffin thing, like the Crystal Palace labyrinthodon, like Coote, like the leaden goddess of the Dunciad, like some fat, proud flunkey, like pride, like indolence, like all that is darkening and heavy and obstructive in life. It is matter and darkness, it is the anti-soul, it is the ruling power of this land, Stupidity. My Kippses live in its shadow. Shalford and his apprenticeship system, the Hastings

Academy, the ideas of Coote, the ideas of the old Kippses, all the ideas that have made Kipps what he is, all these are a part of its shadow. But for that monster they might not be groping among false ideas and hurt one another so sorely; but for that, the glowing promise of childhood and youth might have had a happier fruition, thought might have awakened in them to meet the thought of the world, the quickening sunshine of literature pierced to the substance of their souls, their lives might not have been divorced, as now they are divorced, from the apprehension of beauty that we favoured ones are given—the vision of the Grail that makes life fine for ever. I have laughed, and I laugh at these two people; I have sought to make you laugh. . . .

But I see through the darkness the souls of my Kippses as they are, as little pink strips of quivering living stuff, as things like the bodies of little, ill-nourished, ailing ignorant children, children who feel pain, who are naughty and muddled and suffer and do not understand why. And the claw of this Beast rests upon them! [77]

It remains to note that with *Kipps* Wells attained a secure place among the English humorists. "I'm writing at times with loud guffaws . . . ," he told his agent Pinker. "This book so far is solid comic relief." [78] Bennett was hardly exaggerating when he assured Wells, in a phrase borrowed ironically from the conventional criticism of "the novel of commerce," that there is "a laugh on every page." [79] The novel's early chapters, dealing with Kipps's boyhood, are in the vein of *Tom Sawyer* and *Huckleberry Finn.*

Half-way to the wreck Kipps made a casual irrelevant remark. "Your sister ain't a bad sort," he said off-handedly.

"I clout her a lot," said Sidney modestly, and after a pause the talk reverted to more suitable topics.

Gems of pure absurdity, such as Chitterlow's reiterated claim that his wife has "the finest completely untrained contralto voice in England," abound. But Wells's chief comic resource is Kipps's hopeless vagueness about everything, from the nature of his world to proper English pronunciation. Explaining himself to Chitterlow, for example, he declares, "with the air of one who had seen trouble," "I'm a norfan, both sides." [80]

Of the many hilarious longer sequences in the book, perhaps the most entertaining is Wells's account of Kipps's misadventures as a guest at that splendid London hotel, the Royal Grand. They reach their climax when he wanders one day into the quiet and decorous drawing-room for afternoon tea.

Presently a fluffy, fair-haired lady came into prominent existence a few yards away. She was talking to a respectful, low-voiced clergyman, whom she was possibly entertaining at tea. "No," she said, "dear Lady Jane wouldn't like that!"

"Mumble, mumble, mumble," from the clergyman.

"Poor dear Lady Jane was always so sensitive," the voice of the lady sang out clear and emphatic.

A fat, hairless, important-looking man joined this group, took a chair and planted it firmly with its back in the face of Kipps, a thing that offended Kipps mightily. "Are you telling him," gurgled the fat, hairless man, "about dear Lady Jane's affliction?" A young couple, lady brilliantly attired and the man in a magnificently cut frock coat, arranged themselves to the right, also with an air of exclusion towards Kipps. "I've told him," said the gentleman in a flat, abundant voice. "My!" said the young lady, with an American smile. No doubt they all thought Kipps was out of it. A great desire to assert himself surged up in his heart. He felt he would like to cut in on the conversation in some dramatic way. A monologue something in the manner of Masterman? At any rate, abandoning that as impossible, he would like to appear self-centred and at ease. His eye, wandering over the black surfaces of a noble architectural mass close by, discovered a slot and an enamelled plaque of directions.

It was some sort of musical box! As a matter of fact, it was the very best sort of Harmonicon and specially made to the scale of the Hotel.

He scrutinised the plaque with his head at various angles and glanced about him at his neighbours.

It occurred to Kipps that he would like some music, that to inaugurate some would show him a man of taste and at ease at the same time. He rose, read over a list of tunes, selected one haphazard, pressed his sixpence—it was sixpence!—home, and prepared for a confidential, refined little melody.

Considering the high social tone of the Royal Grand, it was really a very loud instrument indeed. It gave vent to three deafening brays and so burst the dam of silence that had long pent it in. It seemed to be chiefly full of the great-uncles of trumpets, megalotrombones and railway brakes. It made sounds like shunting trains. It did not so much begin as blow up your counter-scarp and rush forward to storm under cover of melodious shrapnel. It had not so much an air as a *ricochette*. The music had, in short, the inimitable quality of Sousa. It swept down upon the friend of Lady Jane and carried away something socially striking into the eternal night of the unheard; the American girl to the left of it was borne shrieking into the inaudible. "High cockalorum Tootle-tootle tootle loo. High cockalorum tootle lootle loo. Bump, bump, bump—BUMP." Joyous, exorbitant music it was from the gigantic nursery of the Future, bearing the hearer along upon its torrential succession of sounds, as if he was in a cask on Niagara. Whiroo! Yah and have at you! The strenuous Life! Yaha! Stop! A Reprieve! A Reprieve! No! Bang! Bump!

Everybody looked round, conversation ceased and gave place to gestures.

The friend of Lady Jane became terribly agitated.

"Can't it be stopped?" she vociferated, pointing a gloved finger and saying something to the waiter about "that dreadful young man."

"Ought not to be working," said the clerical friend of Lady Jane.

The waiter shook his head at the fat, hairless gentleman. People began to move away. Kipps leaned back luxurious, and then tapped with a half crown to pay. He paid, tipped like a gentleman, rose with an easy gesture, and strolled towards the door. His retreat evidently completed the indignation of the friend of Lady Jane, and from the door he could still discern her gestures as asking, "Can't it be stopped?"

The music followed him into the passage and pursued him to the lift and only died away completely in the quiet of his own room, and afterwards from his window he saw the friend of Lady Jane and her party having their tea carried out to a little table in the court.

Certainly that was a point to him. But it was his only score; all the rest of the game lay in the hands of the upper classes and the big hotel. And presently he was doubting whether even this was really a point. It seemed a trifle vulgar, come to think it over, to interrupt people when they were talking.[81]

This is excellent fooling, but parallels to it could be found in the books of Jerome K. Jerome and W. W. Jacobs or in the Grossmiths' delightful *Diary of a Nobody*. What makes Wells more than the chief Cockney humorist of his time is his ability to make such passages integral parts of a serious novel, in which a touching individual history embodies in permanent form the leading social currents of the age. It is on this ground that *Kipps* may be described as the Edwardian *Great Expectations*.

VIII

During the year in which he finished *Tono-Bungay*, Wells wrote a preface to a series of Russian translations of his works, in which is summed up his inspiration for this most ambitious and impressive of his novels:

The literary life is one of the modern forms of adventure. Success with a book—even such a commercially modest success as mine has been—means in the English-speaking world not merely a moderate financial independence but the utmost freedom of movement and intercourse. One is lifted out of one's narrow circumstances into familiar and unrestrained intercourse with a great variety of people. One sees the world. One meets philosophers, scientific men, soldiers, artists, professional men, politicians of all sorts, the rich, the great, and one may make such use of them as one can. One finds oneself no longer reading in books and papers, but hearing and touching at first hand the big discussions that sway men, the initiatives that shape human affairs. . . . The days in the shop and the servants' hall, the straitened struggles of my early manhood, have stored me with vivid memories that illuminate and help me to appreciate all the wider vistas of my later social experiences. I have friends and intimates now at almost every social level from that of a peer to that of a pauper, and I find my sympathies and curiosities stretching out like a thin spider's web from top to bottom of the social tangle.[82]

In *Tono-Bungay* Wells sought to bring together all these impressions. He drew freely from his early life, as he had in *Love and Mr. Lewisham* and *Kipps,* but his focus was on the world in which he currently lived rather than on these memories. His objective was nothing less than to present in a single novel a comprehensive "view of the contemporary social and political system in Great Britain." [83]

To accomplish this spacious aim Wells presented his story as the autobiography of one of his two principals, George Ponderevo, instead of telling it in his own person as he had in his two earlier novels. Thus he contrived to make acceptable *Tono-Bungay*'s loose narrative structure as well as what might otherwise seem an excessive proportion of auctorial commentary. But, as a matter of fact, George is practically Wells's *alter ego*. His childhood, his scientific training, and a large part of his love-involvements parallel Wells's own history. Nor does his skeptical, ironical, generalizing habit of mind, "reaching out into vastly wider issues than our personal affairs," [84] differ from that of his creator.

The "hero" of George's story is his uncle Edward Ponderevo. When the reader first encounters him he is a "little chemist," to all appearances one more ill-educated, ineffectual member of the lower middle class like Kipps or Mr. Polly. But Ponderevo dreams audaciously of "the romance of modern commerce," by which he means vast schemes of monopolistic chicanery made palatable by advertising. His fellow-tradesmen regard his pretensions with contempt, but they fail to understand how thoroughly he is attuned to his world. "One felt that he was silly and wild," George reflects, "but in some way silly and wild after the fashion of the universe." [85]

After failing to make any impression in his country retreat, Ponderevo removes to London, where he soon achieves spectacular success. His "open sesame" is "Tono-Bungay," a patent medicine which he has found in an old book of recipes. "The stuff was . . . a mischievous trash," George confesses, "slightly stimulating, aromatic and attractive, likely to become a bad habit and train people in the habitual use of stronger tonics, and insidiously dangerous to people with defective kidneys." [86] Once "Tono-Bungay" has been established, Ponderevo moves on to a group of "subsidiary specialities," branches out into related fields, and finally embarks on large combinations of firms producing domestic conveniences which make him a famous company promoter.

All this is made possible by advertising campaigns equally remarkable for ingenuity and virulence. "Tono-Bungay Hair Stimulant" is sold by "a little catechism beginning: 'Why does the hair fall out? Because the follicles are fagged.'" "Tono-Bungay Mouthwash" leads to "that inspiring inquiry . . . , 'You are Young Yet, but are you Sure Nothing has Aged your Gums?'" A climax of incongruity is reached when Ponderevo, unable to acquire the *British Medical Journal* or the *Lancet,* buys instead *The Sacred Grove.* This "representative organ of British intellectual culture" is shortly to be seen with a bright new cover, on which appears:

THE SACRED GROVE
*A Weekly Magazine of Art, Philosophy, Science and
Belles Lettres.*

Have you a Nasty Taste in your Mouth?
It is Liver.
You need ONE Twenty-Three Pill.
(Just one.)
Not a Drug but a Live American Remedy.

CONTENTS

A Hitherto Unpublished Letter from Walter Pater.
Charlotte Brontë's Maternal Great Aunt.
A New Catholic History of England.
The Genius of Shakespeare.
Correspondence:—The Mendelian Hypothesis; The Split Infinitive; "Commence," or "Begin"; Claverhouse; Socialism and the Individual; The Dignity of Letters.
Folk-lore Gossip.
The Stage; the Paradox of Acting.
Travel, Biography, Verse, Fiction, etc.

The Best Pill in the World for an Irregular Liver.[87]

Ponderevo is now "the symbol of the age . . . , the man of luck and advertisement, the current master of the world." He becomes a leader among "that multitude of economically ascendant people who are learning how to spend money." [88] A lively chapter recounts his social rise in terms of the houses in which he successively resides. At last nothing will satisfy him but a great mansion of his own building. In preparation for this immense edifice, destined never to be completed, an army of men sets to work, vast hills are moved, and a wall miles long is erected.

These distractions finally involve Ponderevo in financial troubles from which no ingenuity of manipulation can extricate him. When a trial for fraud and forgery impends, George spirits him off by balloon to southern France, where he shortly dies, a frightened and broken man, "his race of glory run and race of shame." He has done society enormous harm,[89] yet the reader finds it difficult to think of him except with forgiving affection. On his deathbed he is the same simple, engaging figure that he had been in earlier exchanges with his nephew:

> "He was an aquarium-faced, long, blond sort of chap, George, with glasses and a genteel accent," he said.
>
> I was puzzled. "Aquarium-faced?"
>
> "You know how they look at you."
>
> . . . .
>
> "It's a great world, George, nowadays, with a fair chance for everyone who lays hold of things. The career *ouvert* to the Talons—eh?" [90]

George's history is presented in counterpoint to his uncle's. He grows up at Bladesover in Kent, a great country estate where his mother is housekeeper. After serving as an assistant in his uncle's chemist's shop, he wins a scholarship to London University. He leaves without a degree to help his uncle in the exploitation of "Tono-Bungay"; but after the success of Ponderevo's enterprises seems assured, he returns to science and engineering, in which he makes a substantial reputation for himself. Meanwhile he has passed through an unsatisfactory marriage and a troubled love affair.

At this point George's story veers into what the reader had come to expect from Wells in his "science fiction." It is surprising enough to find him seeking to make a contribution to the development of lighter-than-air craft through experimentation with balloons. But credence is strained to the breaking point when in a vain effort to save Ponderevo from financial disaster he leads a desperate expedition to a remote island where there are great heaps of "quap," "the most radio-active stuff in the world." In this age of the Geiger counter, when uranium stocks are booming, the "quap" episode has acquired an adventitious realism. Certainly we raise no question when George writes: "Suppose indeed that is to be the end of our planet; no splendid climax and finale, no towering accumulation of achievement but just—atomic decay." [91] But we are still inclined to ask whether Wells would not have done better to rely on quieter plot elements. As the novel ends, George is an engineer for a shipbuilding concern, supervising the construction of destroyers.

The histories of Ponderevo and his nephew are absorbing in themselves, but they acquire far greater interest as the reader is shown how they fit into the "immense process of social disintegration" which is the pattern of contemporary life. Looking back on his career, George finds the essential clue to this pattern in his years at Bladesover.

> The great house, the church, the village, and the labourers and the servants in their stations and degrees, seemed to me . . . to be a closed and complete social system. About us were other villages and great estates, and from house to house, interlacing, correlated, the Gentry, the fine Olympians, came and went. The country towns seemed mere collections of shops, marketing places for the tenantry, centres for such education as they needed, as entirely dependent on the gentry as the village and scarcely less directly so. I thought this was the order of the whole world. I thought London was only a greater country town where the gentlefolk kept town-houses and did their greater shopping under the magnificent shadow of the greatest of gentlewomen, the Queen. It seemed to be in the divine order. . . .

> . . . Bladesover is, I am convinced, the clue to almost all that is distinctively British and perplexing to the foreign inquirer in England and the English-speaking peoples. Grasp firmly that England was all Bladesover two hundred years ago; that it has had Reform Acts indeed, and suchlike changes of formula, but no essential revolution since then; that all that is modern and different has come in as a thing intruded or as a gloss upon this predominant formula, either impertinently or apologetically; and you will perceive at once the reasonableness, the necessity, of that snobbishness which is the distinctive quality of English thought. Everybody who is not actually in the shadow of a Bladesover is as it were perpetually seeking after lost orientations. We have never

broken with our tradition, never even symbolically hewed it to pieces, as the French did in quivering fact in the Terror.[92]

But though England has had no revolution, "this ostensible order has even now passed away." The old aristocracy has in fact abdicated to "the most unpremeditated, subtle, successful and aimless plutocracy that has ever encumbered the destinies of mankind." The result has been to make England the "spectacle of forces running to waste, of people who use and do not replace, . . . a country hectic with a wasting aimless fever of trade and money-making and pleasure-seeking." Once it is understood that the "Bladesover System" is an empty shell, that the new plutocracy is utterly irresponsible, that waste and purposelessness are the leading features of English life, George's experiences and those of Ponderevo assume a thoroughly representative aspect. So George reflects: "All this present commercial civilisation is no more than my poor uncle's career writ large, a swelling, thinning bubble of assurances; . . . its arithmetic is just as unsound, its dividends as ill-advised, its ultimate aim as vague and forgotten; . . . it all drifts on perhaps to some tremendous parallel to his individual disaster." Even the "quap" has its suggestiveness. "It is in matter," George urges, "exactly what the decay of our old culture is in society, a loss of traditions and distinctions and assured reactions." [93]

Wells had concluded *Love and Mr. Lewisham* and *Kipps* with the retreat of his principal characters to an island of domestic content. This solution was not open to George Ponderevo, just as it was not open to Wells himself. Instead George turns to science, as the force that may eventually bring order and purpose into the world, and dedicates himself to this "one enduring thing." [94] But the hope held out for the future by science seems feeble when compared with the tremendous actualities that Wells has described. The dominant impression left by *Tono-Bungay* is that left by Shaw's *Heartbreak House*. It is a picture of a world over which doom impends.

Ranging as it does through past and present and through all levels of English society, *Tono-Bungay* is Wells's supreme effort to embody social forces through individual histories. He considered "A Picture of the World," "One Man's View of England," "The End of an Age," and "Waste," as possible titles, before finally settling on "Tono-Bungay." [95] He was right to choose the thing rather than the abstraction, for the book remains a true novel despite the weight of generalization that it has to bear. One can only agree with Wells's own estimate that it is "his finest and most finished novel upon the accepted lines." [96]

IX

For the last of his four notable novels, *The History of Mr. Polly,* Wells found his starting point in the character of his oldest brother. Frank Wells had been a lively, mischievous boy, whose "natural ingenuity" and mechanical ability made him a neighborhood "leader in his generation." Nine years older than Wells, Frank had not paid much attention to him when he was small; but after Wells reached his 'teens, they became good companions and "had some great holiday walks together." Like all the Wells boys, Frank was apprenticed to a draper. Though hating the work, he put up with it for fifteen years, and then followed Wells's example in breaking away. "He had conceived an ideal of country existence from reading Washington Irving's *Bracebridge*

Hall," Wells writes, and he soon fell permanently into a life of bicycling "about the country, repairing clocks, appreciating character and talking nonsense. If it was not particularly profitable, it was amusing—and free." Despite his "rich humour and imagination," society regarded him as a "complete failure." *The History of Mr. Polly* may be seen as Wells's justification of Frank against the "world of competitive acquisitiveness" in which his gifts were "shoved out of play and wasted altogether." [97]

Wells's novel divides neatly into two movements.[98] We are introduced to Mr. Polly, a short, plump, dyspeptic, ineffectual man approaching forty, as he sits upon a stile surveying his village of Fishbourne and muttering: *"Ole! . . . Oh! Beastly* Silly Wheeze of a hole!"* [99] The first half of the novel is devoted to relating how he has reached this point of utter despair, the second to relating how he escapes from it into happiness. Wells might have borrowed his subject from Gissing, and he treats it as veraciously as that master of dreary realism would have treated it. But he packs every page with humor, and the total effect of the novel, in its movement from black defeat to glorious triumph, is that of heroic romance. In this book at least Wells throws consistency to the winds and joins Kipling in refuting the critics of romance by finding it in everyday life:

> Confound Romance! . . . And all unseen
> Romance brought up the nine-fifteen.

Mr. Polly's life has been one of almost unredeemed disaster. Eight years in the "valley of the shadow" of English education leave him hopelessly confused about nearly everything. He passes another decade clerking in a series of draper's shops, only to find he will never give satisfaction in this line of work. Just when he is about to sink into permanent unemployment, he is rescued by a legacy from his father. After a short breathing spell, he is entrapped into marriage with his cousin Miriam, a constitutionally incompetent, humorless and conventional young woman. Settling with her in a haberdasher's shop in a small southern coastal town, he lives fifteen dreary years, bored with his wife, quarreling with his neighbors, hating his work, and gradually drifting into bankruptcy.

Yet Mr. Polly is a worthy and likable man, loving companionship and endowed with unusual capacity for joy and beauty. "Outside the regions devastated by the school curriculum he is still intensely curious," and he finds reading an unfailing resource, the only thing in fact that makes life bearable. Fed by books, he leads a secret life that anticipates Walter Mitty's:

> He shot bears with a revolver—a cigarette in the other hand—and made a necklace of their teeth and claws for the chief's beautiful young daughter. . . .
>
> He led stormers against well-nigh impregnable forts, and died on the ramparts at the moment of victory. (His grave was watered by a nation's tears.)
>
> He was beloved by queens in barbaric lands, and reconciled whole nations to the Christian faith. . . .
>
> He explored the Amazon, and found, newly exposed by the fall of a great tree, a rock of gold.[100]

This vigorous mental life is outwardly manifested, however, chiefly in his "upside down way of talking." His botched education has made him "uncertain about the spelling and pronunciation of most of the words in our beautiful but abundant and perplexing tongue—that especially was a pity, because words attracted him, and under happier conditions he might have used them well." "New words had terror and fascination for him; he did not acquire them, he could not avoid them, and so he plunged into them." The result is a large but peculiar vocabulary and a tendency towards a nice derangement of epithets. Phrases such as "a bit vulturial," "exploratious menanderings," "melancholic retrospectatiousness," and "benifluous influence" are part of his normal speech. He describes the cheerful and energetic young men who compete with him for employment as "Smart Juniors, . . . full of Smart Juniosity. The Shoveacious Cult." Americans observed in Canterbury leave him with an impression of "Cultured Rapacacity. . . . Vorocious Return to the Heritage." And the sight of his deceased father calls forth: "Second—second Departed I've ever seen—not counting mummies." [101]

In the past when confronted by crises in his affairs, Mr. Polly's only resource has been to mutter "lill dog," as if this were a sufficient explanation and apology, and to disappear.[102] As he sits on his stile, however, he determines for once to take drastic action. He will cut his throat, first setting fire to his shop to avoid trouble for Miriam in collecting his insurance. He bungles this attempt to assert himself, burning up much of Fishbourne while merely nicking himself, but he makes a great discovery in the process. "If the world does not please you, *you can change it.* You may change it to something sinister and angry, to something appalling, but it may be you will change it to something brighter, something more agreeable, and at the worst something much more interesting." [103]

A few weeks later Mr. Polly has quietly disappeared from Fishbourne and is living a serene life as a tramp on the road. One day he comes around a bend of the river to the Potwell Inn and its lawn and garden. "Its deep tiled roof, nestling under big trees —you never get a decently big, decently shaped tree by the seaside—its sign towards the roadway, its sun-blistered green bench and tables, its shapely white windows, . . . its row of upshooting hollyhock plants in the garden, . . . [its] hedge separating the premises from a buttercup-yellow meadow, . . . [and its] three exceptionally tall, graceful, and harmonious poplars" make it an idyllic scene to Mr. Polly. Entering, he finds an equally satisfying interior, presided over by "quite the plumpest woman Mr. Polly had ever seen, seated in an arm chair . . . , peacefully and tranquilly, and without the slightest loss of dignity asleep. . . . She had shapely brows and a straight, well-shaped nose, kind lines of contentment about her mouth, and beneath it the jolly chins clustered like chubby little cherubim about the feet of an Assumptioning Madonna. . . . '*My* sort,' said Mr. Polly." [104] He soon makes himself an indispensable handyman to the plump woman, and becomes the devoted slave of her nine-year-old granddaughter.

But Mr. Polly discovers that this Eden is threatened by a serpent in the person of the plump woman's nephew, Jim, "the Drorback to this place," as she puts it. This powerful and stupid young man has been turned cruel and wicked by years in a reformatory. He has threatened to ruin the plump woman, against whom he has a grudge, and far worse, he has made an impression upon the girl by calling her "the gamest little beast he ever came across," and offering to teach her to swear and spit.

"When Uncle Jim comes back, he'll cut your insides out," she assures Mr. Polly. "P'raps, very likely, he'll let me see." [105]

Jim does not fail to measure up to this description, and when Mr. Polly first encounters him, he is as terrified as is Pip when he meets the convict Magwitch. In the brief period of respite that follows, Mr. Polly knows that his time of judgment has come.

> Life had never been so clear to him before. It had always been a confused, entertaining spectacle. He had responded to this impulse and that, seeking agreeable and entertaining things, evading difficult and painful things. Such is the way of those who grow up to a life that has neither danger nor honour in its texture. He had been muddled and wrapped about and entangled, like a creature born in the jungle who has never seen sea or sky. Now he had come out of it suddenly into a great exposed place. It was as if God and Heaven waited over him, and all the earth was expectation.

He is tempted to run away, to show himself to be in fact the "grumbling, inglorious, dirty, fattish little tramp, full of dreams and quivering excuses," that he seems; but at last he stays to face his destiny.[106]

Three encounters between Jim and Mr. Polly follow, in which the quickness and ingenuity of the one are pitted against the strength and malice of the other. Mr. Polly remains profoundly frightened to the end of his campaign, but he also finds a certain zest in what he is doing. As he dodges away from Jim on one occasion, Wells tells us, "the word 'strategious' flamed red across the tumult of his mind." At last Jim retires defeated. Mr. Polly has proved his manhood, and won a place for himself in the world. Miriam is still a burden on his conscience; but a final visit to Fishbourne reveals that she is better off without him. The fact that he is an arsonist bothers him not at all. "One starts with ideas that things are good and things are bad," he reflects, "—and it hasn't much relation to what *is* good and what *is* bad. I've always been the skepticeous sort, and it's always seemed rot to me to pretend men know good from evil. . . . Most of my time I've been half dreaming. I married like a dream almost. I've never really planned my life, or set out to live. I happened; things happened to me. It's so with every one. . . . There's something that doesn't mind us. . . . It isn't what we try to get that we get, it isn't the good we think we do is good. What makes others happy isn't our trying. There's a sort of character people like, and stand up for, and a sort they won't. You got to work it out, and take the consequences." [107] And on this immoral but satisfactory note, the novel ends.

In contrast to *Kipps* and *Tono-Bungay*, Wells makes little effort in *The History of Mr. Polly* to explain the broad social implications of his story. In part this is owing to the limited scope of the novel, which clearly does not afford the opportunities for comment presented by Wells's earlier books. But a more important reason for Wells's avoidance of intervention is the perfection with which his social theme is assimilated in Mr. Polly's history. Wells wants to show the human waste involved in society's treatment of "that vast mass of useless, uncomfortable, under-educated, under-trained, and altogether pitiable people" who make up the lower middle class.[108] But no amount of sociological description can begin to convey this message as effectively as does a living picture of Mr. Polly that brings out both the limitations under which he has to live and his possibilities once freed from these limitations. Hence V. S. Pritchett's observation that "Pollyism is as definite a state of mind as Bovaryism was and a more agreeable." [109]

The History of Mr. Polly has always been Wells's best-loved novel, and a few distinguished admirers, among them Sinclair Lewis,[110] have argued that it is also his best novel. We have seen that Wells himself rated *Tono-Bungay* highest, but he did call *The History of Mr. Polly* "his happiest book and the one he cares for most." [111]

x

In 1908 Wells had expressed the hope that he might write "novels and novels only for some years to come." [112] *Kipps* and *Tono-Bungay* had brought him both critical and popular success, and he was widely regarded as the leading novelist of his generation. But his success had aroused resentment as well as admiration. His personal life left him vulnerable to attack, and the underlying radical animus of his novels had not escaped the censure of conservative critics. A reaction set in when he published two careless stories, *Ann Veronica* (1909) and *The New Machiavelli* (1911), in which he gave offense respectively by his unconventional views concerning sexual morality and by his satirical portraits of contemporary celebrities. There was an unsuccessful press boycott of these books engineered by "a group of eminent and influential persons" who were conducting "an organized attempt to suppress Wells." [113] This experience left him unamenable to any sort of discipline, literary or otherwise, and anxious to hit his enemies hard. "Just at present I don't like the world I live in," he told an interviewer in 1911, "and I'm not disposed to say I do like it. I feel as though I was living in a stuffy, slovenly room full of noisy and violent people. All sorts of storms, boycotts, censorships and foolishness prevent me opening the windows and letting in a little air and sanity." [114]

Moreover, as Wells noted, the campaign against him had lent his work "an enormous, unpremeditated popularity. . . . I have been given an artificial and exaggerated importance. I have become a symbol against the authoritative, the dull, the presumptuously established, against all that is hateful and hostile to youth and to-morrow. They have thrust youth and to-morrow into my undeserving hands." [115] Here was an opportunity too good to miss for furthering his "open conspiracy" on the part of men of good-will "to correlate the intelligence, will and conscience of the individual to the social process." [116]

But his new public wanted novels from Wells, not sociological treatises. He accordingly set himself to writing fiction of frankly propagandistic intent, of which there are substantial anticipations in *Ann Veronica* and the latter half of *The New Machiavelli*. So it came about that with *Marriage* (1912), *The Passionate Friends* (1913), *The Wife of Sir Isaac Harman* (1914), *The Research Magnificent* (1915), and *Mr. Britling Sees It Through* (1916), Wells turned to the "Novel of Discussion," the leading feature of which is long exchanges among the characters on social questions of topical interest. Chaffery, Chitterlow, Masterman, and Ewart in his earlier books had been persons "of quite unequalled gift for monologue," [117] but Wells had been at pains to confine their speeches to a chapter or two, to relate them directly to the novel's main theme, and to keep them entirely in

character. In these later fictions, on the other hand, the mono-
logists are given their heads and take over the book, in the
process destroying it as a novel.

Thus it happened that Wells, as James noted in 1912, "cut loose
from literature clearly—practically altogether." [118] He had forgotten the lecture on the difference between the reformer and
the novelist which he had read to Grant Allen sixteen years
earlier. He ignored Conrad's admonition to make his art "contain his convictions, where they would be seen in a more perfect
light." [119] When he did revert to his former manner in *Bealby*
(1915), he gave the book the significant subtitle "a Holiday,"
and produced an acrid though still amusing farce which cannot
be compared with *Kipps* or *The History of Mr. Polly*. His
adoption of the "dialogue novel" had forced his final abandon-
ment of the literary ideals which he had held for fifteen years.
Indeed, he came to take a kind of pleasure in insisting that he
was a journalist and a philistine, interested only in getting on
with the world's work in a rough-and-ready way. Yet a wistful
note sometimes crept into his references to the period when he
devotedly pursued "the Novel," and "in extreme old age he was
sometimes heard to say: 'Someday, I shall write a book, a *real*
book.' " [120]

XI

The Edwardian age was a period of sociological preoccupations.
Galsworthy's early novels from *The Island Pharisees* to *The
Patrician* illustrate the prevailing concern for social generaliza-
tion; so too do Bennett's *Clayhanger* and Forster's *Howard's
End*. But Wells in the four books which we have been consider-

ing was by far the most ambitious and successful anatomist of the Edwardian social order in fiction. He was also the last English novelist to write from a sense of society as a whole, perhaps because after the First World War English society became so fluid and unstable as to make its summarization in general terms impossible.

This achievement is impressive because Wells managed also to be a remarkably accomplished novelist on traditional lines in *Love and Mr. Lewisham, Kipps, Tono-Bungay,* and *The History of Mr. Polly.* As V. S. Pritchett has remarked: "In all of his books, even the poor ones, Wells has always started with this power to bounce; in early novels like *Mr. Polly* and *Kipps* he went on bouncing; he had us lightly but completely in his hands."[121] Wells doubted whether even these books had "that sort of vitality which endures into new social phases." He thought that "in the course of a few decades . . . the snobbery of Kipps . . . or the bookish illiteracy of Mr. Polly may be altogether inexplicable."[122] He has done his work as a novelist so well, however, that these characters remain as much alive as ever. Moreover, a new social setting has not suppressed snobbery; and no one who has taught freshman English in an American university would claim that Mr. Polly's sort of bookish illiteracy has disappeared.

It is my conclusion, then, that during his great years as a writer Wells not merely tried to be "a Novelist," he succeeded. And when one considers how substantial is his accomplishment in his scientific romances, in his short stories, and in his *Experiment in Autobiography,* which Professor Jack Isaacs has shown some cause for regarding as "in many ways the most important of twentieth century books," [123] as well as in the novel proper, it is hard to deny him a rank in Edwardian literature just below that of Conrad, James, Yeats, and Shaw, however much Wells himself in his later phase as prophet and publicist may have sought to forswear his accomplishments as a man of letters.

The Edwardian Theater and the Shadow of Shaw

GERALD WEALES

Of all the terminal dates in English drama—except 1642, of
course—1914 puts the most emphatic full stop to an era. Since
the First World War there has been no cohesive English drama
movement. There was an embryonic gesture toward a political
theater in the 1930s and a more successful religious drama revival which has determinedly worked its narrow vein. There have
been remarkable individuals—James Bridie, for instance—and
festivals, although these thrive on tourism as much as on the
theater. There has been the whisper of a school with John
Osborne and his even younger contemporaries, but what is missing in English theater, and has been missing since Edwardian
days, is a recognizable face and form. The Edwardian drama
is so palpable a unit that it might almost be held in one's hand
—or one's handbook—its outlines and eccentricities as clear—for
all the differences among individuals—as those of the Elizabethan
theater. The Edwardian theater that concerns us here is not that
of Beerbohm Tree or Lewis Waller or George Edwardes and his
Gaiety Girls; it is the comparatively large body of still readable,

still produceable plays, written by those playwrights, whether for the commercial or the little theater, who believed that the play is, if not *the* thing, at least *a* thing not to be sacrificed to the whimsies of a matinee idol. There are three primary identification marks of this Edwardian drama: (1) its sense of expectation which has become, for us, a fact of achievement; (2) its faith in the theater as an institution that might transcend its box office; and (3) its acceptance of an implied exchange of ideas between the theater and the social, political, and psychological world in which it made its way. All three of these are, in a sense, the marks of George Bernard Shaw, the shadow that he threw on his contemporaries.

The expectation for the English theater was part of a general Edwardian pattern which assumed that intelligence and determination, coupled with sound committee work, could perform wonders even in an impractical world. Later, after optimism had died on the battlefields of France, Shaw could look back at Heartbreak House and recognize the decay behind the Edwardian façade, but at the turn of the century, he, like so many others, faced the future confidently and was willing to spend his breath and his energy toward shaping it to his ends. The hope for the theater was that the advanced or intellectual drama—as it was variously called, often to the distaste of its practitioners [1]— would eventually find a permanent place for itself in English theater, that it would finally come to compete successfully with the sentimental comedies and romantic dramas that were the chief attractions of the West End. One evidence of this hope was the boundless talk about the future of the theater. In the pages of the *English Review* and the *Fortnightly Review,* men like Granville Barker and St. John Hankin used the prospect of an endowed theater or the bogey of the Censorship as an excuse to dwell on the kind of theater that they hoped one day to see flourish.[2] Their remarks were sprinkled, consciously one supposes, with echoes of the Shaw criticism that had appeared in the *Saturday Review* in the late nineties and of which a selection was published in 1906. More important than the talk were the practical tools with which the experimentalists hoped to hack their way into the marketplace. Of these the two most important were the Stage Society and the Granville Barker–J. E. Vedrenne seasons at the Court Theatre, 1904–7, and Shaw was very much a part of both operations. He served as the first chairman of the Stage Society's producing committee and provided it with its first play, *You Never Can Tell;* he was not only the leading playwright of the Court Theatre, he was also its chief financial backer and, judging from the recently published Shaw-Barker letters, its most determined critic, complainer, and idea man.

It might be argued that these operations were no more than a provincial echo of the growth of modern European drama, that what Barker and Vedrenne tried to do at the Court was only a pale and finally unsuccessful attempt to follow in the footsteps of the Théâtre Libre and the Freie Bühne, that J. T. Grein had already made the experiment a decade earlier with the Independent Theatre, that what was happening in London was happening also in Dublin, Manchester, and Birmingham. All that is true, of course. Yet, the important thing to anyone interested in English drama is that it was now happening in London. It was not enough to recognize a new kind of drama abroad, not enough to import it—against opposition—into England. That the expectation implicit in the Court Theatre could not succeed on its own terms is finally beside the point; theatrical rebels carry the day not at the box office but in the history of the theater. They make it possible for others to follow and to do easily and successfully, in commercial terms, what they have done with difficulty and with pain. Lady Peckham, in Granville Barker's *The Secret Life,* which is set in the early 1920s, says, "Twenty years back, if we'd known it, was our time for a good revolution." Had she narrowed her generalization to the theater alone, she would have had to admit—if Barker's still fresh scars from those years would have let him admit—that the revolution had taken place. With the success of Shaw in the first decade of this century, modern drama had finally come to England. The Edwardian dramatists, who thought of themselves as pioneers, were not opening up new land; they were building solid structures—often of imported material—on the ground where the antiquated cabins of Robertson, Pinero, and Jones had stood.

Except for Somerset Maugham—and even he was momentarily afflicted by a sense of cause—the playwrights of the Stage Society and the Court Theatre—Barker and Hankin, John Galsworthy, John Masefield, Arnold Bennett—thought of themselves as a vanguard with Shaw as the acknowledged (or occasionally unacknowledged) leader. "For our drama is renascent," wrote Galsworthy, "and nothing will stop its growth. It is not renascent because this or that man is writing, but because of a new spirit."[3] A complement to the sense of impending triumph was the belief, implied in Galsworthy's "new spirit," that there was something worth triumphing about. As a group, these playwrights believed that the theater, once it was freed of the necessity to manufacture vapid entertainment for empty minds, could reclaim the spiritual, the inspirational, the pedagogical function which rightly belonged to an institution which shared common origins with the church. Shaw was kidding seriously in 1906 when he wrote:

> A theatre to me is a place "where two or three are gathered together." The apostolic succession from Eschylus to myself is as serious and as continuously inspired as that younger institution, the apostolic succession of the Christian Church.[4]

If the Edwardian playwrights, half in earnest, accepted Shaw's portrait of the poet as priest, they were as much concerned— still following Shaw—with the practical problems of getting ideas on stage in ways that were both amusing and exciting. Still, amusement and excitement (about nothing, it is true) were the staples of the West End, and although the new playwright hoped not to lose these elements in his plays, his first concern had to be with ideas if his theater was to be inspirited in a way that would make it a valid part of the modern society in which it sought position and relevance.

In the narrowest sense, in plays like Elizabeth Robins's *Votes for Women!,* immediate social problems were examined, but the bulk of the Edwardian playwrights followed Shaw in forwarding "advanced ideas," by which they meant simply the old artistic idea that there should be some exchange between art and society, between art and nature. This, I suppose, is what John Galsworthy had in mind when he said that that "new spirit" of his "in the main rises from an awakened humanity in the conscience of our time."[5] It is certainly what Shaw had in mind when, unhappy at the way the *Pygmalion* rehearsals were going, he wrote to Mrs.

Patrick Campbell: "I give up in despair that note of terror in the first scene which collects the crowds and suddenly shews the audience that there is a play there, and a human soul there, and a social problem there, and a formidable capacity for feeling in the trivial giggler of the comic passages." [6] Within that single sentence lies not only a definition of Shavian drama, but of the aims of the playwrights around Shaw: to make some comment on genuine human beings, to offer some recognition of the importance of social context—the intellectual drama made flesh, so to speak.

There was no one way of doing that. The less imaginative, of whom Galsworthy was the most imaginative, attempted to build narrowly naturalistic structures able to bear "a spire of meaning." [7] St. John Hankin tried to filter the conventional "society drama" through his wry and sometimes bitter comic imagination. John Masefield searched out a regional realism which was essentially as romantic as all that business about going down to the sea again. Whatever the method, each of them, like Shaw, was intent on confounding the simple-minded attitude that St. John Hankin describes in "A Note on Happy Endings":

> Our dramatic critics when they enter a theatre seem to leave all sense of reality outside and judge what they see there by some purely artificial standard which they would never dream of applying to the fortunes of themselves or their friends. To them all engagements are satisfactory and all marriages are made in Heaven, and at the mere thought of wedding bells they dodder like romantic old women in an almshouse. No wonder they have reduced our drama to the last stage of intellectual decrepitude.[8]

Not that the new drama was dogmatically adverse to the happy ending. The biggest hit of the Court seasons, Shaw's plays aside, was *Prunella,* the harlequin play that Granville Barker wrote with Laurence Housman. But, here, what in a contemporary setting would have been conventional became traditional; the pleasure in it may have been that of any play about the triumph of love, but the conception was intellectual. Ideas would creep in; the Shavian infection did spread. Nor could the best of the West End playwrights escape the influence. Granville Barker, who called *The Professor's Love Story* "about as cynically bad a play as any man of its author's calibre could expect to write," insisted that J. M. Barrie, beginning tentatively with *The Wedding Guest,* changed himself from a mere hack to a good playwright. Barker's examination of Barrie's plays in *The Bookman* [9] was not only a nod of respect to a craftsman, it was also—though never specifically—a recognition that Barrie, for all his easy success, was one of *them,* that the best of the Edwardian dramatists, commercial or experimental, were a kind of family. Shaw, of course, was father.

That Shavian shadow that fell across Edwardian drama was a shadow in more ways than one. It not only marked the plays of the period by coloring the playwrights with Shaw's idea of the theater, it ended by obscuring the other dramatists almost completely. I have tried to suggest in the summary above that Edwardian drama not only constitutes a recognizable body of work, but that within that body there is a larger group of still acceptable plays than at any other comparable period in modern English drama. This contention seems to me easily demonstrable. As

Dame Edith Sitwell said to the young lady who wanted to know how to understand her poems, "Read them, my dear, read them." [10] If you accept, with me, that there is a high degree of quality in the Edwardian plays and want to verify that such acceptance is not common, try—as I did when I first began to think fondly of the period—to convince a few publishers that an anthology of Edwardian plays would be desirable.

Of the playwrights of the period, only J. M. Barrie and John Galsworthy can be said to have held on to reputations among the nonspecialists. *What Every Woman Knows* and *Dear Brutus* are still done frequently, on and off television, and some of the other Barrie plays occasionally achieve production; *Quality Street,* for instance, became a musical, *Dear Miss Phoebe,* in 1950. Still, I cannot help feeling that Barrie has survived largely by turning himself into Peter Pan. Galsworthy is still a staple of student anthologies, but that is probably because a Galsworthy play, like the M-1 rifle, can be dismantled and reassembled easily for purposes of demonstration; even so, he has disappeared from some of the latest collections.[11] The Maugham who is still read and occasionally performed is not the Edwardian Maugham but the playwright of the 1920s. Granville Barker and the Edwardian Pinero briefly claimed places for themselves in the larger anthologies, but now, although Barker is in paperback, he is there as a Shakespeare critic and an expert on education and the theater, and Pinero, if he is mentioned at all, is likely to be considered as the *farceur* of the 1880s.

The chief cause of this comparative decline is Shaw himself. As early as 1907, St. John Hankin, while ostensibly reviewing Shaw's dramatic criticism, could say: "Mr. Shaw is indisputably the most distinguished living English dramatist. He is, in fact, the only dramatist of world-wide reputation whom we have." [12] The context of Hankin's statement indicates that it may have been more disputable than his assurance implied; he aimed his declaration at the heads of these critics who still treated Shaw's plays "with a contemptuous impatience that they would never dream of displaying to those of Mr. Grundy or Captain Marshall." Shaw's triumph of the Edwardian years lay as much with his attackers as with his supporters. Both groups of critics came to use Shaw as a touchstone, as an inevitable point of comparison. That critical habit survived the First World War and is with us still. Since Shaw is one of the only two playwrights that England has contributed to the world's major dramatists, he quite naturally outgrew his contemporaries. Ordinary playwrights, even good ones, look insignificant alongside giants. The bulk of the Edwardian plays could be saved only by the kind of major surgery that was performed by the scholars who cut Shakespeare loose from his Elizabethan competitors. Although it might be profitable to consider the ways in which Shaw was an Edwardian and the ways in which the Edwardian theater was Shavian, it would be kinder to the other playwrights if Shaw would go off quietly to Parnassus and allow us to see the groundling playwrights on their own.

I do not intend extensive excavations in this paper. Let Barrie and Maugham lie quietly, stirred by occasional winds that blow in from the box-office. Let someone else exhume Hankin or Masefield. I have not even the inclination to say kind words about Galsworthy because I find myself agreeing with Humbert Humbert that he is "a stone-dead writer of sorts." [13] Of all the playwrights of the period, the one that most deserves attention is Granville Barker. Barker was in so many ways a shadow of Shaw—if I may finally kick that shadow conceit to death—that he has never received the attention that his quality demands. For all that he absorbed from his friendship with the older playwright, his few plays are distinctively personal—in their achievements and in their shortcomings. I would like to spend the rest of this paper dislodging Barker from the Shavian context and considering him as a dramatist in his own right. A thorough examination of Barker would have to consider his collaborations; his adaptations; his early and fascinating *The Marrying of Ann Leete,* which places the nineteenth-century new woman in the late eighteenth century; his two plays of the 1920s, *The Secret Life* and *His Majesty,* which were apparently never acted; his later revisions of the Edwardian plays (the last version of *The Voysey Inheritance* was not done until 1934). There is not space here for so complete a study. I will give my attention to the three plays, all with contemporary settings, written between 1903 and 1909—*The Voysey Inheritance, Waste,* and *The Madras House.* These three plays not only give ample indication of Barker's ideas and his theatrical techniques, they are also his best work and the most impressive plays, Shaw's aside, to come out of England during the Edwardian years.

Barker was, theatrically speaking, a kind of three-headed monster. He came into the new century, at twenty-two, with a decade's experience as an actor and with at least one playwriting credit to his name. A special matinee performance of *The Weather-hen,* which he wrote with fellow-actor Berte Thomas, had been given at Terry's Theatre on June 29, 1899. The third head was added shortly after the century had turned when Barker directed three one-acters for the Stage Society. It was the Society that brought Shaw and Barker together. Since Barker was connected, as actor or director, with most of the society's productions in the first half of 1900, Shaw presumably knew him and his work, but the close friendship between the two men did not begin until Barker played Marchbanks in the society's revival of *Candida* in July of that year. By December, Shaw was able to write Barker, warning him not to play Captain Brassbound in the society production of Shaw's new play: "Your divine gifts of youth, delicacy and distinction will be murdered; and so will the part." [14] The ironic exaggeration that marked so much of Shaw's correspondence was already apparent in his notes to Barker; so was the affection masked as exasperation, the high praise disguised as a simple demand for his due, the sound advice pretending to be slapstick. In this case, Barker settled for the part of Captain Kearney. Within the next few years, Barker created such important Shavian characters as John Tanner in *Man and Superman,* Adolphus Cusins in *Major Barbara,* and Louis Dubedat in *The Doctor's Dilemma.* The playbills and the reviews of the period testify to the connection between Shaw and Barker as an actor; the relation between Shaw and Barker as a director is less easy to clarify. Since Shaw insisted on directing his own plays, Barker is listed as director only on the Stage Society production of *The Admirable Bashville* in 1903, the two revivals at the Savoy in 1907, and the first presentation of *Androcles and the Lion* in 1913. Even so meager a list of Barker credits is misleading. Shaw had a way of turning up when a production was nearly finished and taking over from the ostensible director in order to give the play the authentic Shavian touch; he also, as the Shaw-Barker letters indicate, had a way of bombarding the nominal director with post cards full of good advice. The influence, however, was not all in one direction. Although Shaw was in charge of his own plays when they were done at the Court Theatre, Barker, as artistic director of the whole Court venture, often as leading actor, always as close friend, must certainly have had a share in the final form that the Shavian productions took—so great a share, in fact, that C. B. Purdom suggests that he should be listed as co-director.[15]

Acting and directing are such ephemeral activities—at least, they were until the motion picture came in—that any discussion of the mutual influence of Shaw and Barker is lost in intangibles unless it settles on their writing. Barker as a playwright was obviously affected by Shaw, but he did not write Shavian plays. In structure, in characterization, in dialogue, he was his own man, or if he owed allegiance to anyone, it was to Ibsen, not to Shaw. Barker's obvious artistic independence should not be confused with ideational self-sufficiency. The force of Shaw's ideas, even of his idiosyncrasies, was so great on the younger man that in the early years of their friendship Barker became a Fabian and a vegetarian. There are Shavian echoes in many of the Barker plays. Ann Leete and Alice Maitland suggest, palely, the Shavian managerial women, and freebooting old Mr. Voysey might be one of Shaw's strong men. Philip's decision at the end of *The Madras House* to stand for County Council, "to do dull, hard work over drains and disinfectants," obviously owes something to Shaw's years as vestryman in the Borough of St. Pancras and to his Fabian belief that practical work on specific problems is more important than ideational attitudinizing. The analyses of the family, of social relationships, of economic structure, of political conventionality that are at the heart of Barker's plays are marked by Shaw's views, but in the end the diagnoses become Barker's own, become, in fact, more detailed and more subtle than those in Shaw's plays. Barker absorbed much from Shaw, but absorption is not mimicry. It is Barker's individuality and not his similarity to Shaw that is most impressive.

The two things about Barker's plays that have always struck reviewers forcibly, and often unpleasantly, is his apparent indifference to conventional plot and his insistence on protagonists who could only look disconcerted if they were asked to wear the label "hero." The apparent problem of plot in Barker is that there is not enough of it; the actual problem is that there is too much. A. B. Walkley, in a review in the *Times,* has spoken for the opposition:

> It must be difficult to write a play in four acts, four fairly long acts, the last in two scenes, and throughout them all to keep your audience blankly ignorant of the meaning of it. Many of those persons who sat throughout *The Marrying of Ann Leete* at the Royalty Theatre yesterday afternoon must have wished it were impossible.[16]

What Walkley missed in *Ann Leete,* apparently, and what others have found missing in the later Barker plays, is an easily apprehendable line of action. A great deal seems to be going on in Barker's plays—certainly a great deal is being said—and, yet, those who demand the impact of events are likely to come away from the plays with the impression that nothing has happened. In *The Voysey Inheritance,* Edward Voysey at first grudgingly, finally willingly takes over the legacy of swindling left him by his father. In *Waste,* Henry Trebell commits suicide when, after Mrs. O'Connell has killed herself to keep from having his baby, he is forced out of a shadow government and faced with the defeat of the education bill in which he believes. In *The Madras House,* the owners of a once famous dressmaking establishment sell out to an American. Of these three plays, only *Waste* would seem to fill the conventional idea of a plot, but even it turns perversely against the sentimental notions of theatrical action by making Mrs. O'Connell's death finally irrelevant to the dismissal of Trebell and by refusing to propound a simple cause-and-effect reason for the final suicide. All three of my one-line descriptions are inaccurate, of course, for each one of the Barker plays is peopled with a great number of characters, each of whom is sufficiently developed to suggest that he has a life (that is, a plot) of his own. Often such a character appears briefly and disappears and his immediate relevance to what might as well be called plot is not clear. Ethel Voysey, for instance, whom we see only in Act Two of *The Voysey Inheritance,* dies in childbirth between Acts Three and Four and her death has nothing to do with Edward's decision about carrying on his father's swindling in the hope of setting his inequities right. As Ethel and similar characters in the other plays indicate, Barker is not interested in telling the conventional stage story.

Nor is he interested in the conventional stage hero. "Keep your worms for your own plays," Shaw once wrote to Barker, "and leave me the drunken, stagey, brassbowelled barnstormers my plays are written for." [17] Barker's leading characters are all introspective and a little self-pitying. They must learn, in some way, to cope with a society which refuses to be organized in its own best interests—which means in the image that the protagonists have built of what a society should be—or, like Henry Trebell, they must leave it. Edward Voysey discovers that he can only begin to operate effectively by shedding his ideas, which have made him an intellectual prig, and Philip Madras accepts that there is a moment in which a man must cease to long for the big changes and begin to work for the small ones. C. B. Purdom has suggested [18] that all of the Barker protagonists—even Ann Leete—are self-portraits, that their difficulties at adjustment were Barker's own. There may be something to this biographical approach to the plays, for Barker's career is one of false starts and dead ends, but if so, Barker's self-images are relatively unimportant. His protagonists are not heroes; they are hardly even leading characters. The decisions that Edward Voysey, Henry Trebell, and Philip Madras are forced to make are the conclusions of their plays, not the culminations; the processes by which they reach their decisions are simply the strings on which the plays are hung. Barker *is* indifferent to plots and to heroes; his plays are organized on quite another principle.

If analogies from music were a little less precious in literary criticism, one might say that each of the Barker plays introduces a theme and works variations on it. At least, each of them is primarily concerned with seeing all around a particular idea or social attitude. In *The Voysey Inheritance,* for instance, the inheritance appears, at first glance, to be simply the legacy of swindling that passes to Edward from his father and which

Mr. Voysey had received, in his turn, from the founder of the firm. This simple definition of the inheritance dissolves early in the play. In the first place, Mr. Voysey's account of how he became involved is ambiguous and, after his death, still other versions of the story come to Edward. The one thing that is clear is that Mr. Voysey took a delight in his swindling, found in it a challenge and an excitement that could not have come to him as an ordinary solicitor. Intelligence and nerve were necessary, after all, for a man to manipulate so many different trust funds, to use their capital for his own purpose, without ever being caught short. At first, Edward takes part to protect his father and, then, after Mr. Voysey's death, to salvage the capital of some of the small holders. By Act Four, he is able to answer his brother Hugh's question, "What do you gain by hanging on now?" with the single word "Occupation." By the last act he is willing to admit, pressed by Alice Maitland, who has kept him at the job, that his father's legacy has made a man of him. It becomes clear that Mr. Voysey has left Edward more than an ugly situation; he has given him a chance to escape his youthful platitudes, to discover his capabilities when faced with an untidy, nontheoretical bit of life.

There are other Voysey inheritances, too. So much of the play deals not with Edward's problems, but with the rest of the Voyseys—a comfortable, slightly smug, English middle-class family whose position depends on the money that Mr. Voysey has stolen over the years. No picture of English middle-class family life of the period is as complete and as damning as the one that Granville Barker gives in this play. The family scenes display a genuine, if exasperated, affection among the members; at the same time they show how each of the children is, in his own way, a victim of the family. Honor, the eldest child, shunted aside when sons came, has become a spinster and a kind of glorified housekeeper. Booth, the third son, went into the army and has become a blustering major who is, in fact, a receptacle for all of the English sentimental clichés about home, country, and mother. Hugh, the youngest son, is a failed artist in whom middle-class philistinism struggles with a genuine desire to rebel; it is Hugh who says of the eldest son, Trenchard, who broke with the family completely, that he escaped "From tyranny! . . . from hypocrisy! . . . from boredom! . . . from his Happy English Home!" The Voysey family is, then, part of the Voysey inheritance—both the sentimental surface that Booth celebrates and the destructive reality that lies beneath.

If the titular inheritance of this play seems to imply so many different things—there is, of course, the real money that Mr. Voysey leaves to his children—the complications are few when one comes to think of the varieties of waste in the play of that name. At the end of that play Walter Kent, Henry Trebell's young secretary, is given this curtain speech: "No, I don't know why he did it . . . and I don't care. And grief is no use. I'm angry . . . just angry at the waste of a good man. Look at the work undone . . . think of it! Who is to do it! Oh . . . the waste . . . !" The waste that upsets Walter, that a brilliant, still-young man should have destroyed himself when there was so much that he might have done, is the simplest kind of waste that Barker touches on. Throughout the play it is clear that the party politicians are leery about using a man like Trebell, who has more intelligence than party loyalty, with the implication that the English political system is designed to waste its best brains. Trebell's suicide hangs on more than his disappointment over the inevitable defeat of his education plan; Mrs. O'Connell's death has killed both his child, which she was carrying, and his idea, which the party leaders reject in rejecting him. This stifling of his two avenues of creativity leads to his suicide, but not until he has gone back into himself and has discovered his own insufficiency. In having built a life on complete rationality, in having reduced the emotional to the biological, he has destroyed the possibility of love in himself. His desire to help man in the abstract is no substitute for human affection and he comes to think that he has wasted one whole side of a man's potentiality.

Mrs. O'Connell, a flirt whose only assets are physical, wastes herself by her fear of bearing a child and, through her suicide, wastes the unborn baby. The other women in the play are victims of another kind of waste. The English political and social system is not able to make direct use of the minds of its women. So Miss Trebell has taken second best by being a teacher and then by becoming housekeeper to her brilliant brother; Mrs. Farrant has tried to be a political woman through her husband, and Lucy Davenport will try to do the same thing through Walter Kent. "What's a woman to do?" Lucy asks Henry Trebell. "She must work through men, mustn't she?" There are also the kinds of waste that worried Henry Trebell—the waste of undereducated children, the waste of the religious impulse when it was directed toward no social good and the practical waste of the money that would come from disestablishment if the government frittered it away on unplanned benefits. In the face of so extended a use of the play's title, Walter Kent's lament about the waste of a man becomes ironic; its rightness only points up its inadequacy to an understanding of the situation.

In *The Voysey Inheritance* and *Waste,* Barker plays with his themes almost as though his titles were conceits that were there for the juggling. In *The Madras House* the thematic method is used more directly; the pretense of a story is gone. Philip Madras is present in each of the four acts and he does reach a personal decision at the end of the play, but it is impossible to think that anyone could be concerned about Philip and his decision, certainly not to the extent that Edward Voysey and Henry Trebell demand our allegiance. *The Madras House* is an explicit examination of English sexual behavior, and each of the four acts, whose only connection is Philip, examines either the sexual implications of a particular social situation or a variety of attitudes to the marital and extra-marital customs of society in general. In this clinical decade, when sexual relations have ceased to be the relations between sexes and have become simply a matter of mechanics, Barker's play may seem tepid to the academic pornographer. It is, in fact, one of the subtlest examinations we have of the relations of men and women in a society which binds the communication between sexes in economic and social restrictions. Much of the detail of the play is specifically Edwardian, but many of the general attitudes and a large number of the particular instances still have validity today.

The first act presents the Huxtables, an English family reminiscent of the Voyseys, but with six unmarried daughters. With a domineering mother, an ineffectual but miserly father, and English middle-class ideas about what constitutes a suitable marriage, most of the girls have already passed the age of possibility. Laura, like Honor Voysey, has dwindled to housekeeper; Minnie and Clara have taken to religion; there are still elements of rebellion, not quite stifled, in the other three. An exchange between Philip and Emma, the most sensible of the girls, indicates what lies just under the surface of their comfortable Edwardian home:

> *Emma.* I say . . . I suppose I oughtn't to tell you about Julia, but it is rather a joke. You know, Julia gets hysterical sometimes, when she has her headaches.
>
> *Philip.* Does she?
>
> *Emma.* Well, a collar marked Lewis Waller came back from the wash in mistake for one of father's. I don't think he lives near here, but it's one of those big steam laundries. And Morgan the cook got it, and she gave it to Julia . . . and Julia kept it. And when mother found out she cried for a whole day. She said it showed a wanton mind. (*Philip's mocking face becomes grave.*)
>
> *Philip.* I don't think that's at all amusing, Emma.
>
> *Emma.* (*In genuine surprise.*) Don't you?
>
> *Philip.* How old is Julia?
>
> *Emma.* She's thirty-four. (*Her face falls, too.*) No . . . it is rather dreadful, isn't it?

As though having finished with the small, controlled experiment of the Huxtable household, repression on the domestic scale, Barker turns in Act Two to the offices of Roberts and Huxtable, a drapery firm allied to the Madras House, in which the many sins of the living-in system are examined. Miss Chancellor, the company housekeeper, represents the kind of professional virgin —I am not using the term in the contemporary slang meaning

—who is so necessary to such a firm, whose self-righteousness allows her to exalt her own lack of inclination and opportunity into a moral dictum. The Brigstocks, whose secret marriage is withering because Mr. Brigstock is afraid to ask company permission to live outside, are, for Barker, victims of the economic system, although he chooses to display them through the relationship most suitable to the play's theme—the marriage that has made Mrs. Brigstock a jealous hysteric. "I lie awake at night away from him till I could scream with thinking about it," she says at one point. "And I do scream as loud as I dare . . . not to wake the house. And *if* somebody don't open that window, I shall go off." Her outburst comes in the middle of a meeting in which Philip must serve as peacemaker, must assure the couple that no one really believes Miss Chancellor's accusation that Mr. Brigstock is the father of the child Marion Yates is carrying. The artificiality of the situation in which they all live is so great that Miss Chancellor's experience, as an observer, has let her build a sequence of imaginary events on the basis of a single kiss of friendship. Marion Yates is the typical new woman of the Edwardian plays; like Janet in St. John Hankin's *The Last of the De Mullins,* which had appeared two years before, Marion acts practically to defeat the double standard. She chooses to have an affair and plans to have the child on the assumption that her ability to earn a living frees her from the necessity of marriage. Marion is contrasted not only to the Brigstocks and Miss Chancellor, but also to Philip Madras's wife, who appears briefly at the end of the act. Jessica is educated, elegant, poised, but, unlike Marion, she falls unthinkingly into the role that society seems to have chosen for her. She not only flirts with her husband, but also with Philip's friend, Major Thomas, who wishes that she would not be so attentive to him and counters Philip's "She doesn't want to be made love to," with "Yes, she does. I don't mean that unpleasantly . . . but all women do. Some of 'em want to be kissed and some want you to talk politics . . . but the principle's the same." The device of the living-in system might have dated this act completely if Barker had not taken the trouble to use it metaphorically as well as realistically; it becomes clear that Jessica Madras, who acts as Major Thomas expects, and Thomas, who reacts as Jessica expects, are as bound by society and economics to their sexual roles as are the unprotesting victims of the living-in system.

The third act is a wonderfully ironic discussion of the English woman. Ostensibly a business meeting in which arrangements are made for the selling of the Madras House, it is actually a display of a wide range of male sexual attitudes. Major Thomas is the casual polygamist who feels guilty about it, and Constantine Madras, Philip's father, the founder of the Madras House, who has long since left England to live in the Near East, is the practicing polygamist who is proud of it. Constantine and Major Thomas share a condescension toward women which becomes, in Constantine's mouth, a rationalization for his inability to treat a woman as anything but a servant and a sexual object. Mr. Huxtable is the gentle monogamist who becomes suspicious that he has been used all his life as a convenience, as Constantine's women have. Philip is the intellectually advanced man—he would have gone to the Duke of York's to see *The Madras House*—who does not understand why women cannot be treated and cannot expect to be treated simply as people. The funniest portrait of the lot, although the strokes may be a little too broad, is that of the American, Eustace Perrin State, who has come to buy the firm. He is a man who speaks ennobling abstractions about women from the safe redoubt of bachelordom; he sees his mission as one which will let the English middle-class women break into a world of beauty, although he incidentally points out that "they form one of the greatest Money-Spending Machines the world has ever seen." He describes, with some pride, an experiment in his Nottingham shop in which the men's wear department is staffed by attractive women and the women's wear by handsome men—"Always, of course, within the bounds of delicacy"—and in which business has greatly improved. This genteel prostitution underlies the whole scene. Against the abstract talk of women, Windlesham, the effeminate manager of the Madras House, introduces French models wearing the latest importations, one of which is copied from a famous courtesan, another of which is called, by Constantine, an aphrodisiac.

In the fourth, the summary act, Constantine is seen briefly with his wife and victim, Philip's mother, and as victim of Marion Yates's desire for a child. Finally Philip and Jessica attempt to discuss intelligently what she calls "that farmyard world of sex." For the most part, and rightly, the discussion is a quarrel. Although anthropologists have taught us that sexual mores are tied to societal attitudes, the gentle positive approach of Philip, his decision to give up the Madras House for the County Council on the assumption that he should try to change such attitudes, not to cater to them, is no solution. Barker sensibly cuts off Jessica's last speech in mid-sentence; "She doesn't finish," says the stage direction, "for really there is no end to the subject." The strength of *The Madras House* for us is that, despite the Edwardian exterior, the furnishings are contemporary.

When a playwright's approach is as determinedly intellectual as Barker's is in these three plays, there is a danger that characterization may be sacrificed to the illustrated lecture. For the most part, Barker escapes that danger. Occasionally, as with Marion Yates, a character becomes too conventionally propagandistic, but even she is saved from being a cliché of the advanced theater by Barker's mixing her high principles with a touch of little-girl rebellion. A few of the characters approach recognizable stage stereotypes, but in such cases Barker ordinarily pulls himself up short, as he does with Mrs. Voysey, who avoids being simply an absent-minded old lady by virtue of the scene in which with amiable ruthlessness, she tells the family that she has always known about Mr. Voysey's swindling and that her own money has been kept untouchably separate. Even the most casual character in a Barker play is given the kind of definition that will let one place him socially, economically, and ideationally, and, as likely as not, a hint of personal motivation will be added to suggest what moves the external labels he wears. The leading characters are constructed from their actions and their speeches, of course, but more importantly from the variety of impressions of them that one gets from the other characters. To Mr. Huxtable, for instance, Philip Madras is the young man deserting the family business; to the Huxtable girls he is the cousin they have always known; to the Brigstocks he is that unfathomable person, the employer; to his father, he is something of a fool; to his wife, he is dangerously like his father. These are only a few of the Philips that we glimpse in *The Madras House*. This coming at a character from all directions tends to give him as many faces as real people have. Sometimes, however, Barker works differently, letting a single line put an otherwise consistent character into a new perspective. For most of *The Voysey Inheritance,* Alice Maitland is the strong-minded girl whose idealism is tempered by practicality, but this image is consistently nagged by a line that comes from Hugh's wife, who has known poverty; when Alice says, "There's a joy of service," Beatrice reacts with "I forgot . . . you've four hundred a year?"

The care with which Barker makes each of his characters an individual is matched by his concern to provide a fitting milieu. He is no occupational regionalist, reporting on the clan habits of solicitors or the millinery trade, but he communicates, more surely than any other playwright of the period, a genuine sense of profession. For so many playwrights, the occupational label is no more than a convenience; the Reverend Morell in *Candida,* for instance, might have been in any charismatic trade. Although Barker is never primarily interested in the details of the way in which a character earns his living, he is aware that a man's personality depends in part on his profession and he is, therefore, careful to make Mr. Voysey, say, a believable solicitor. Compare, for instance, the two soliciting firms in *The Voysey Inheritance* and *Justice.* Galsworthy, like Barker, is intent on occupational verisimilitude and so he sprinkles the managing clerk's room in James How's offices with tin boxes and estate plans; he is careful with the details of pass-books and counterfoils. Yet, the Hows seem to be in business simply to provide an occasion for poor Falder to forge a check and, then, to provide specimen attitudes

—unrelenting in James's case, more forgiving in Walter's— toward the crime. In *The Voysey Inheritance,* although Edward's dilemma is the main concern, Barker manages with only a few details to suggest an entire structure of investment, the relation of one trust to another, the difference between a safe investment and one that may bring a higher yield; he manages this through Mr. Voysey, for these, after all, are Mr. Voysey's chief concerns, at least while he is in the office. I cannot say how accurate Barker is in his depiction of the soliciting firm or of the millinery business, but Voysey and Son, Roberts and Huxtable and the Madras House have an almost tangible reality that comes largely from the fact that Barker's characters, despite the way the playwright uses them thematically and they use themselves emotionally, are in- escapably bound up in their businesses. Perhaps the best example of detailed professional realism comes in the gathering of the politicians in Act Three of *Waste;* although Barker makes quite clear that personal prejudice tempers principle, that expediency and ineptitude counter intelligence, his politicians remain be- lievable, even sympathetic men, quite in contrast to the caricatures with whom Shaw plays in *Back to Methuselah.*

The social settings, like the professional, have every appearance of reality. In fact, Barker's ability to open a real drawing-room door and turn us loose in a genuine social group may be a draw- back to the casual audience. Only a saving irony keeps Act One of *The Madras House* from being as boring to the reader as it is to the characters; the Huxtables, put on their good behavior by finding a stranger in their midst, make polite conversation, repeat introductions endlessly, and only occasionally come alive when family quarrels peek through the social façade. The act, which builds to a crescendo of fifteen polite good-byes, is actually very funny, although the author's satirical intention is not immediately perceivable where the bromides gather as the act begins. The first act of *Waste* is as carefully conceived as that in *The Madras House,* and it, too, provides its difficulties. As in so many Edwardian plays, we are taken into a drawing-room where the ladies are gathered; in Mrs. Farrant's drawing-room, however, unlike the standard theatrical one, nothing is explained. The air is full of allusions to people who are not identified and to events that are not described; the audience comes, like a guest at a party where everyone, including the host, is a stranger to him, and it takes most of the act to find one's ways through what is being said. By the end of the act, the characters begin to take form as individuals, the general direction of the action is indicated, a few of the kinds of waste have been touched on, but the audience has had to work for what it has received and very few members of an audience like to have demands made on them.

Those things that I find most admirable about Barker—his subtlety, his intellectuality, his many-sided characterizations, the strange mixture of irony and sympathy with which he approaches men—are probably the qualities that kept him from being a widely successful playwright in his own day and sent him into the relative obscurity which has been his since then. They are also the qualities that would make profitable a reawakened interest in him. Barker's plays have their weaknesses, of course, and in some ways—the involvement with disestablishment in *Waste,* for instance—they are dated. The virtues, however, far outweigh the defects. No serious Edwardian playwright, least of all Barker, escaped the influence of Shaw, but Barker, more than any other dramatist of the period, suffered from too close an identification with the older playwright. It is time that his plays received serious consideration on their own and obvious merit; it is time for Barker to step out of the shadow of Shaw.

Two Faces of Edward

RICHARD ELLMANN

Victoria stayed too long, Edward arrived too late. By the time the superannuated Prince of Wales became king, it was evident that a change would take place in literature; it took place, but Edward has somehow never received credit for it, and the phrase Edwardian literature is not often heard. We have to fall back on it, though, because there is no neat phrase in English, like "the nineties," to describe the first ten years of a century. The word Edwardian has taken its connotations from social rather than literary history. Just what it means is not certain, beyond the high collars and tight trousers which flouted Victorian dowdiness then, and which now have become the pedantic signs of juvenile delinquency. Perhaps "pre-war courtliness" is the closest we can come to the meaning of Edwardian outside literature, sedate Victorianism in better dress. The meaning was present enough to Virginia Woolf for her to declare that "on or about December 1910," that is, in the year of Edward's death, "human character changed." [1] Edward "the Peacemaker" had to die before the world could become modern, and she pushed the dead Edwardians aside to make room for the lively Georgians. The distinction was more relevant, however, for describing Virginia Woolf's own accession to purposiveness than George's accession to rule.

While the late Victorians seem to have relished the idea that they were the last, the Edwardians at once declined to consider themselves as stragglers, ghostly remains of those Englishmen who had stretched the empire so far. The Edwardians had, in fact, a good deal of contempt for the previous reign, and an odd admiration for their own doughtiness. In the midst of the general melancholy over Victoria's death, her son said sturdily, "The King lives." [2] To Virginia Woolf the hated Edwardian writers were Bennett, Galsworthy, and Wells, yet even these writers labored under the apprehension or misapprehension that they were trying something new. Lascelles Abercrombie, in one of the few essays on Edwardian literature, finds the period to be only the decorous extension of tradition, and in his essay is detectable that faintly patronizing note which occurs also in biographies of Edward that prove the king was a worthy man.[3] So for Abercrombie the writers of this time were engagingly discreet; they drew in literature, as Edward in life, upon an ample wardrobe, and perhaps dared to go so far as to leave unbuttoned the lowest button on their literary waistcoats.

That the Edwardians have been discounted is understandable, I think, because of the prevalence of a sociological assumption. If the birth of modern literature is dated back to the century's first decade, what happens to our conviction that it was the Great War which turned the tables? At any cost we have to confine the beginning of the century to the infancy or adolescence of modern writers, so that only when the guns boomed did they become old enough to discern the nature of the world. The admonitory fact, however, is that most of the writers whom we are accustomed to call modern were already in their twenties or older when King Edward died. In 1910 Eliot was twenty-two, Lawrence and Pound were twenty-five, Joyce and Virginia Woolf were twenty-eight, Forster was thirty-one, Ford Madox Ford thirty-seven, Conrad fifty-three, Shaw fifty-four, Henry James sixty-seven. Bennett, Galsworthy, and Wells were in their forties. To dismiss most of the writers I have named as either too young or too old to be Edwardians, as if only men of middle age counted in literary fashion, is one of those historical simplicities like denying that the twenties were the twenties because so many people didn't know the twenties were going on. Neither age nor self-consciousness determines the private character of a period; if anything does, it is the existence of a community between young and old experimental writers. Such a community existed in the Edwardian period. It was a community which extended not only across the Irish Sea but, spottily at least, across the Channel and the Atlantic; so, if I extend Edward's dominions occasionally to countries he did not rule, it is only to recover the imperial word Edwardian from an enforced limitation.

If a moment must be found for human character to have changed, I should suggest that 1900 is both more convenient and more accurate than Virginia Woolf's 1910. In 1900, Yeats said with good-humored exaggeration, "everybody got down off his stilts; henceforth nobody drank absinthe with his black coffee; nobody went mad; nobody committed suicide; nobody joined the Catholic Church; or if they did I have forgotten." [4] That there was pressure upon them to change was something that the writers of this time were distinctly aware of; it is not only Yeats, whose attitudes, as Mr. Whitaker has shown, take a new turn; it is also lesser writers. Even John Masefield was once asked how it had happened that his poetry had moved from the nostalgic rhythms of his early work to the more athletic ones of "The Everlasting Mercy," and he replied simply, "Everybody changed his style then." The Edwardians came like Dryden after Sir Thomas Browne, anxious to develop a more wiry speech. Their sentences grew more vigorous and concentrated. I will not claim for the Edwardians' work total novelty—that can never be found in any period, and many of their most individual traits had origin in the nineties or earlier. But in all that they do they are freshly self-conscious. What can be claimed is that there was a gathering of different talents towards common devices, themes, and attitudes, and King Edward at least did nothing to impede it.

What strikes us at once about Edwardian literature is that it is thoroughly secular, yet so earnest that secularism does not describe it. It is generally assumed that in this period religion was something to ignore and not to practice. Edwardian writers were not in fact religious, but they were not ostentatiously irreligious. In the Victorian period people had fumed and left the churches; in the Edwardian period, becalmed, they published memoirs or novels describing how strongly they had *once* felt about the subject. This is the point of Gosse's *Father and Son* (1907) as well as of Samuel Butler's *The Way of All Flesh* (written earlier, but published in 1903). It was also part of the subject of Joyce's *A Portrait of the Artist as a Young Man*, much of it written in 1907-8, as it is of Yeats's first autobiographical book, *Reveries over Childhood and Youth*, written just before the war. In all these books the intensity of rebellion is past, an incident of an unhappy childhood (and the vogue of having had an unhappy childhood may well have begun with the Edwardians) succeeded by confident maturity.

Because they outlived their passionate revolt, writers as different as Yeats and Joyce are sometimes suspected nowadays of having been reverted Christians or at least demi-Christians. Certainly they no longer make a fuss about being infidels. And they are suspected of belief for another reason, too. Almost to a man, Edwardian writers rejected Christianity, and having done so, they felt free to *use* it, for while they did not need religion they did need religious metaphors. It is no accident that the Catholic modernists, with their emphasis upon the metaphorical rather than the literal truth of Catholic doctrines, became powerful enough in the first years of the century to be worth excommunicating in 1907. There were other signs of a changed attitude toward religion: the comparative mythologists tolerantly accepted Easter as one of many spring vegetation rites; William James's *The Varieties of Religious Experience,* published in 1902, made all varieties equally valid.

In creative writers, this new temper appears not in discussion of religion, which does not interest them, but in vocabulary. Religious terms are suddenly in vogue among unbelievers. Yeats calls up God to be a symbol of the most complete thought. Joyce allows the infidel Stephen to cry out "Heavenly God!" when, seeing a girl wading, he experiences "an outburst of *profane* joy." [5] Elsewhere, as in *Ulysses,* he asks what difference it makes whether God's name be Christus or Bloom, and Jesus is allowed into *Finnegans Wake* as one of Finnegan's many avatars. Ezra

Pound, newly arrived in London in 1908, immediately writes a canzone to celebrate "The Yearly Slain," a pagan god, and then a ballad to celebrate the "Goodly Fere," who turns out to be Christ made into a Scottish chap. All deaths of all gods roused Pound to the same fervor. There was no need to attack with Swinburne the "pale Galilean," or to say with Nietzsche that "God is dead"; as a metaphor God was not dead but distinctly alive, so much so that a character in Granville Barker's play *Waste* (1906–7) asks sardonically, "What is the prose for God?" [6] T. S. Eliot, if for a moment he may be regarded as an Edwardian rather than as a Rooseveltian, used John the Baptist and Lazarus in "Prufrock" (written in 1910), as if they were characters like Hamlet, and even in his later life, after becoming consciously, even self-consciously Christian, he used the words "God" and "Christ" with the greatest circumspection, while unbelievers used the words much more casually, their individual talents more at ease in his tradition than he himself. D. H. Lawrence, the same age as Pound, writes his "Hymn to Priapus" in 1912, yet remains attracted by images of Christ and is willing enough, in spite of his preference for older and darker gods, to revise Christianity and use its metaphors. In *The Rainbow* (begun the same year), Tom Brangwen and his wife, when their physical relationship improves, experience what Lawrence variously calls "baptism to another life," "transfiguration," and "glorification." [7] In later life Lawrence would give Christ a new resurrection so he could learn to behave like the god Pan, and in poems such as "Last Words to Miriam" the cross becomes emblematic of the failure to cohabit properly, an interpretation which I should like to think of as Edwardian or at least post-Edwardian. Even H. G.

Wells played for a time with the notion of a "finite God," "the king of man's adventures in space and time," though in the end he granted, too unimaginatively, that he had been guilty of "terminological disingenuousness." [8]

To accept Christianity as one of a group of what Gottfried Benn calls "regional moods," or to rewrite it for a new, pagan purpose, seemed to the Edwardians equally cogent directions. For the first time writers can take for granted that a large part of their audience will be irreligious, and paradoxically this fact gives them confidence to use religious imagery. They neither wish to shock nor fear to shock. There is precision, not impiety, in Joyce's use of religious words for secular processes. About 1900, when he was eighteen, he began to describe his prose sketches not as poems in prose, the fashionable term, but as "epiphanies," showings-forth of essences comparable to the showing-forth of Christ. *Dubliners* he first conceived of in 1904 as a series of ten *epicleseis,* that is, invocations to the Holy Spirit to transmute bread and wine into the body and blood of Christ, a sacramental way of saying that he wished to fix in their eternal significance the commonplace incidents he found about him. To moments of fullness he applied the term "eucharistic." When Stephen Dedalus leaves the Catholic priesthood behind him, it is to become "a priest of eternal imagination, transmuting the daily bread of experience into the radiant body of everlasting life." [9] One did not have to be a defected Irish Catholic to use terms this way. Granville Barker's hero in *Waste* wants to buy the Christian tradition and transmute it.[10] Proust, searching for an adjective to express his sense of basic experiences, calls them "celestial." [11] Yeats, a defected Protestant, wrote in 1903, as Mr. Whitaker reminds us, that his early work was directed toward the transfiguration on the mountain, and his new work toward incarnation. The artist, he held, must make a Sacred Book, which would not be Christian or anti-Christian, but would revive old pieties and rituals in the universal colors of art instead of in the hue of a single creed.

The reestablishment of Christianity, this time as outer panoply for an inner creed, was not limited to a few writers. In the Edwardian novels of Henry James the words he is fondest of are "save" and "sacrifice," and these are secular equivalents for religious concepts to which in their own terms he is indifferent. In the novels of E. M. Forster, mostly written before Edward died, there is exhibited this same propensity. Forster usually reserves his religious imagery for the end of his novels. In the last pages of *Where Angels Fear to Tread,* his first novel (1905), Forster writes of Philip, "Quietly, without hysterical prayers or banging of drums, he underwent conversion. He was saved." [12] *The Longest Journey* (1907) concludes with Stephen Wanham undergoing "salvation." [13] In *A Room with a View* (1908), there is a "Sacred Lake," immersion in which, we are told, is "a call to the blood and to the relaxed will, a passing benediction whose influence did not pass, a holiness, a spell, a momentary chalice for youth." [14] At the end the heroine derives from Mr. Emerson, who has "the face of a saint who understood," "a sense of deities reconciled, a feeling that, in gaining the man she loved, she would gain something for the whole world." [15]

Even allowing that writers always incline to inflated language for their perorations, Forster obviously intends his words momentously, almost portentously. He is not for Christ or Pan, but with profoundly Edwardian zeal, for the deities reconciled.

Some of the same images appear with much the same meaning in his contemporaries. A character in Granville Barker calls for "A secular Church." [16] Shaw's *Major Barbara* (1905) makes similar use of the theme of salvation with its earnest fun about the Salvation Army. Let us be saved, Shaw says, but with less Christian noise and more Roman efficiency. Forster's "chalice" is like the chalice in Joyce's *Araby* (written in 1905), which is a symbol of the boy's love for his sweetheart. The "Sacred Lake" with its subverting of Christian implication is like *The Lake* in George Moore's novel (1905), in which the priest-hero immerses himself in the lake not in order to become Christian, but to become pagan. Forster's deflection of familiar Christian phrasing in having his heroine feel that, in gaining the man she loves she gains something for the whole world, is cognate with Joyce's heroine in "The Dead" (written in 1907), who says of her pagan lover, "I think he died for me," [17] a statement which helps to justify the ending of that story in a mood of secular sacrifice for which the imagery of barren thorns and spears is Christian yet paganized. I do not think it would be useful to discriminate closely the slightly varying attitudes towards Christianity in these examples: the mood is the same, a secular one.

Yet to express secularism in such images is to give it a special inflection. The Edwardians were looking for ways to express their conviction that we can be religious about life itself, and they naturally adopted metaphors offered by the religion they knew best. The capitalized word for the Edwardians is not God but life: "What I'm really trying to render is nothing more nor less than Life," says George Ponderevo, when Wells is forty-three; [18] "Live," says Strether to Little Bilham, when Henry

James is sixty; [19] "O life," cries Stephen Dedalus to no one in particular when Joyce is about thirty-four; [20] "I am going to begin a book about Life," announces D. H. Lawrence, when he is thirty. [21] It does not much matter whether life is exciting or dull, though Conrad is a little exceptional in choosing extraordinary incidents. Arnold Bennett is more usual in his assurance that two old women are worth writing *The Old Wives' Tale* (1908) about. The Edwardians vied with each other in finding more and more commonplace life to write about, and in giving the impression of writing about it in more and more common speech. In Ireland there is the most distinct return to simple men for revelation, in the peasant drama, in Lady Gregory's collection of folklore, in Moore's and Joyce's short stories; but there is a good deal of it in England too, in Arthur Morrison for example. It is connected with an increasing physicality in writers like Lawrence and Joyce, as if they must discuss the forbidden as well as the allowed commonplace. In Lawrence and in Yeats there is the exaltation of spontaneous ignorance, the gamekeeper in the one and the fisherman in the other held up as models to those who suppose that wisdom is something that comes with higher education. In 1911 Ford Madox Ford calls upon poets to write about ash-buckets at dawn rather than about the song of birds or moonlight. [22] While Henry James could not bring himself to joy in ash-buckets, he too believed that by uninhibited scrutiny the artist might attract life's secrets.

The Edwardian writer granted that the world was secular, but saw no reason to add that it was irrational or meaningless. A kind of inner belief pervades their writings, that the transcendent is immanent in the earthy, that to go down far enough is to go up. They felt free to introduce startling coincidences quite flagrantly, as in *A Room with a View* and *The Ambassadors,* to hint that life is much more than it appears to be, although none of them would have offered that admission openly. While Biblical miracles aroused their incredulity, they were singularly credulous of miracles of their own. As Conrad said in *The Shadow-Line,* "The world of the living contains enough marvels and mysteries as it is; marvels and mysteries acting upon our emotions and intelligence in ways so inexplicable that it would almost justify the conception of life as an enchanted state." [23] The central miracle for the Edwardians is the sudden alteration of the self; around it much of their literature pivots. In 1907 Yeats began work on *The Player Queen,* a dramatic statement of his conviction that, if we pretend hard enough to be someone else, we can become that other self or mask. That was the year, too, when Joyce planned out the miraculous birth of his hero's mature soul as the conclusion of *A Portrait of the Artist,* and when John Synge, in *The Playboy of the Western World,* represented dramatically the battle for selfhood. At the end of Synge's play, Christy Mahon is the true playboy he has up to now only pretended to be, and his swagger is replaced by inner confidence. In *The Voysey Inheritance* (1905) Granville Barker brings Edward Voysey to sudden maturity when, like the hero of that neo-Edwardian novel *By Love Possessed,* he discovers the world is contaminated and that he may nonetheless act in it. Lawrence's heroes must always shed old skins for new ones. In Conrad's *Lord Jim* (1900), the struggle for selfhood is the hero's quest, a quest achieved only with his death. In Henry James's *The*

Ambassadors (1903), the miracles among which Strether moves at first are phantasmagoric, but there is no phantasmagory about the miracle which finally occurs, the release of Strether from ignorance to total understanding. Though the dove dies in another of James's novels of this time (1902), her wings mysteriously extend beyond death into the minds of the living, to alter their conduct miraculously. The golden bowl (1904) is cracked and finally broken, but by miracle is re-created in the mind.

Miracles of this sort occur in surprising places, even in H. G. Wells. In *Kipps* the hero is transformed from a small person named Kipps into a bloated person named Cuyps and finally into a considerable person named Kipps. He is himself at last. Less obviously, such a change takes place in George Ponderevo in *Tono-Bungay*. It is part of Wells's favorite myth of human achievement, and trying to express that George Ponderevo says, "How can I express the values of a thing at once so essential and so immaterial?"[24] To do so he falls back upon the words "Science" or "Truth," words as reverberant for Wells as "chalice" for Forster or "eucharist" for Joyce. Selfhood—the crown of life, attained by a mysterious grace—forced the Edwardians into their grandest metaphors. It will not seem strange that Bernard Shaw's mind hovers continually about it, as in *Man and Superman* (1901–3) and *Pygmalion* (1912), where miracles as striking and as secular as those in Synge, Joyce, or Yeats, take place. Perhaps we could distinguish two kinds of such miracles: the kind of Shaw and Wells, in which a victory in the spirit is accompanied usually by some material victory, and the kind of James, Lawrence Conrad, Yeats, and Joyce, in which a victory in the spirit is usually accompanied by some material defeat. Shaw complained vigorously to Henry James that James's kind of miracle was not "scientific." [25]

If the secular miracle is usually the climax of Edwardian writings, there is also a thematic center, usually some single unifying event or object, some external symbol which the Edwardians bear down upon very hard until, to use Conrad's unprepossessing phrase, they "squeeze the guts out of it." [26] So Forster's *A Room with a View* is organized around the title; Lucy Honeychurch, viewless at first, must learn to see; Forster plays upon the word "view" at strategic points in the novel, and at the end Lucy attains sight. In Conrad's *Nostromo* (1904) the central motif is silver, established, by Conrad's custom, in the first chapter: silver civilizes and silver obsesses, a two-edged sword, and the different attitudes that silver inspires control the action of the book. The meaning of the hero's name, Nostromo, becomes as ambiguous as silver; a lifetime of virtue is balanced against an ineradicable moral fault, and Nostromo dies an example of Conrad's fallen man, partially at least saved by misery and death. In *The Man of Property* (1906), John Galsworthy, somewhat under Conrad's influence, developed the very name of Forsyte into a symbol, and as if fearful we might miss it, he keeps reminding us that the Forsytes were not only a family but a class, a state of mind, a social disease. The use of a symbolic nucleus in these books seems to justify itself by its public quality, a whole society being measured in terms of it. In *The Golden Bowl,* one of those demonstrations of method which Forster found too extreme, Henry James not only invokes the bowl itself several times in the novel, but keeps invoking its atmosphere by repeating the words "gold" and "golden." Verbal iteration is a means by which Edwardian novelists make up for the obliquity of their method, the complexity of their theme, and give away some of their hand. So Conrad in *Lord Jim* speaks of his hero's clothing, on the first page, as "immaculate," and at the last he is "a white speck," all the incongruities of the book pointed up by the overemphasis on stainlessness. Joyce plays on a group of words in *A Portrait,* "apologise," "admit," "fall," "fly," and the like, expanding their meaning gradually through the book. The pressure of this Edwardian conception of novel-writing is felt even in the work of Lawrence. In his first book, written in 1910, Lawrence is still rather primitive in his use of key words. He changed his title from *Nethermere* to *The White Peacock,* and then laboriously emphasized his heroine's whiteness and introduced discussion of the pride of peacocks. By the time he started *The Rainbow* two years later, he had developed this technique so far as to use the words "light" and "dark," and the image of the rainbow itself, obsessively, and he does not relax this method in *Women in Love* or his later books. He even does what most Edwardians do not do, writes his essay "The Crown" to explain what light, dark, and rainbow signify.

A good example, too, is Joyce's transformation of *Stephen Hero* (1904–5) into *A Portrait of the Artist as a Young Man* (chiefly 1907–8). Between writing the two books he read a good deal of Henry James, George Moore, and others, and quite possibly caught up Edwardian habits from them. *Stephen Hero* was to a large extent a Victorian novel, with an interest in incident for its own sake; so Joyce was particularly pleased when he composed the scene in which Stephen asks Emma Clery to spend the night with him. But two or three years later he expunged that scene: it had become irrelevant to his central image. For by then he had decided to make *A Portrait* an account of the gestation of a soul, and in this metaphor of the soul's growth as like an embryo's he found his principle of order and exclusion. It gave him an opportunity to be passionately meticulous. In the new version the book begins with Stephen's father and, just before the ending, it depicts the hero's severance from his mother. From the start the soul is surrounded by liquids, urine, slime, seawater, amniotic tides, "drops of water" (as Joyce says at the end of the first chapter) "falling softly in the brimming bowl." The atmosphere of biological struggle is necessarily dark and melancholy until the light of life is glimpsed. In the first chapter the fetal soul is for a few pages only slightly individualized, the organism responds only to the most primitive sensory impressions, then the heart forms and musters its affections, the being struggles towards some unspecified, uncomprehended culmination, it is flooded in ways it cannot understand or control, it gropes wordlessly toward sexual differentiation. In the third chapter shame floods Stephen's whole body as conscience develops; the lower bestial nature is put by. Then, at the end of the penultimate chapter, the soul discovers the goal towards which it has been mysteriously proceeding—the goal of life. It must swim no more but emerge into air, the new metaphor being flight. The last chapter shows the soul, already fully developed, fattening itself for its journey until at last it is ready to leave. In the final pages of the book, Stephen's diary, the style shifts with savage abruptness to signalize birth. The soul is ready now, it throws off its sense of imprisonment, its melancholy, its no longer tolerable conditions of lower existence, to be born.

By making his book the matrix for the ontogeny of the soul, Joyce achieved a unity as perfect as any of the Edwardians could achieve, and justified literally his description of the artist as like a mother brooding over her creation until it assumes independent life. The aspiration towards unity in the novel seems related to the search for unity elsewhere, in psychology for example, where the major effort is to bring the day-world and the night-world together. Edwardian writers who commented on history demonstrated the same desire to see human life in a synthesis. In 1900 Joyce announced in his paper on "Drama and Life" that "human society is the embodiment of changeless laws," [27] laws which he would picture in operation in *Finnegans Wake*. H. G. Wells insisted later that "History is one," [28] and proceeded to outline it. Yeats said, "All forms are one form," and made clear in *A Vision* that the same cyclical laws bind the lifetime of a person, a civilization, or an idea; and this perception of unity enabled him, he said, to hold "in a single thought reality and justice." [29]

When they came to state their aesthetic theories, the Edwardians bore down hard on the importance of unity. To choose one among a multitude of their sources, they were to some extent making English the tradition of the *symbolistes* of whom Arthur Symons had written in 1899. Aggressively and ostentatiously, the Edwardians point to their works as microcosms characterized by the intense apprehension of the organic unity of all things. They felt justified in subordinating all other elements to this node of unity. Events of the plot can be so subordinated, for example, since, as Virginia Woolf declares, life is not a series of gig lamps symmetrically arranged but a "luminous halo." [30] Short stories and novels begin to present atmospheres rather than narratives; and even when events are exciting in themselves, as in Conrad and often in James, the artist's chief labor goes to establish their meaning in a painstaking way, and he will often set the most dramatic events offstage or, rather than present them directly, allow someone to recollect them. Time can be twisted or turned, for unity has little to do with chronology. What subject matter is used becomes of less importance because any part of life, if fully apprehended, may serve. As Ford Madox Ford says in describing the novel of this period, "Your 'subject' might be no more than a child catching frogs in a swamp or the emotions of a nervous woman in a thunderstorm, but all the history of the world has gone to putting child or woman where they are. . . ." [31] Since characters are also subsidiary to the sought-after unity, there is a tendency to control them tightly. Few Edwardian characters can escape from their books. Galsworthy's plays are called *Strife* (1909) or *Justice* (1910), as if to establish the preeminence of theme over character. The heroic hero is particularly suspect. He is undermined not only by Lytton Strachey in *Eminent Victorians* (1912), but by Joyce, who calls his first novel *Stephen Hero* as if to guard by irony against Stephen's being really heroic; Granville Barker, as Mr. Weales has shown, writes plays in which the heroes do not deserve the name. The Edwardian male, as he appears in the books of this time, is often passive and put upon, like Maugham's Philip in *Of Human Bondage* (published in 1915 but drafted much earlier) or James's Strether, not only because this is the period of the feminist movement, but because it is the period of the hero's subordination. Concurrently, there is a loss of interest in what the hero does for a living—the emphasis comes so strongly upon their relatively disinterested mental activity that the occupations of Strether, Birkin, or Bloom become shadowy and almost nominal.

The amount of unity which the Edwardians instilled in their work is one of their extraordinary accomplishments. As Edith Wharton aggressively and seriously declared in the *Times Literary Supplement* in 1914, "the conclusion of [a] tale should be contained in germ in its first page."[32] Conrad said in his preface to *The Nigger of the "Narcissus"* that a work of art "should carry its justification in every line."[33] There were occasional signs of revolt against this zealous "desire and pursuit of the whole."[34] So Wells found Henry James's insistence upon what he apply called "continuous relevance" to be objectionable.[35] "The thing his novel is about is always there," he said disapprovingly,[36] probably remembering how Joseph Conrad had irritatingly asked several times what Wells's own novels were really *about*.[37] Wells thought himself later to be in favor of irrelevance, but as Gordon Ray points out, he himself said that "almost every sentence should have its share in the entire design," and his best books are not thoughtlessly constructed; they are unified, as I have suggested, by the myth of selfhood.

The Edwardian aesthetic is fairly closely related to the imagist movement, or part of it. T. E. Hulme had interested Pound and others in his theory of intensive manifolds, that is, of wholes with absolutely interpenetrating parts instead of aggregates of separate elements. Hulme instructed them to place themselves "inside the object instead of surveying it from the outside." [38] This position was that which Yeats also insisted upon when he said that the center of the poem was not an impersonal essence of beauty, but an actual man thinking and feeling. He threw himself into the drama because he saw in it a rejection of externality, even of scenery, and an invitation to the writer to relinquish his self. Henry James was also convinced that the "mere muffled majesty of irresponsible 'authorship' " [39] must be eliminated, and entered the consciousness of his most sensitive characters so thoroughly as to make possible disputes over where *he* stood.

What is confusing about the first imagist manifestoes is that this theory has got mixed up with another, a notion of objectivity and impersonality which, though it receives passing applause from Stephen in *A Portrait,* is not Joycean or Edwardian. Most Edwardian writing is *not* aloof, and the poems Pound praised for their imagist qualities were poems like Yeats's "The Magi," or Joyce's "I hear an army," in which the writer is not at all removed from his image. Pound found a more congenial version of the Edwardian aesthetic in the vorticist movement, for that was manifestly based upon the absorption of the artist into his work, rather than his detachment from it. The word "vortex" was something of an embarrassment. Pound said, with an obvious allusion to its female symbolism, "In decency one can only call it a vortex." [40] But it had the advantage of implying the death of the poet in his poem: the ultimate arrogance of the artist is to disappear. This was the point of view of James and of Yeats as well as of Joyce; Edwardian writers were not much concerned with the artist as were writers of the nineties; they were concerned only with the art. They began to put away their flowing ties. Yeats could never understand the reluctance of some writers to let him improve their poems for them, since to him the work was all. The Edwardian writer is an artist not because he proclaims he is, as Wilde did, but because his works proclaim it. There is much less time for affectation and eccentricity, the point being to get on with the job. As Conrad said in his preface to *The Secret Agent,* "In the matter of all my books I have always attended to my business. I have attended to it with complete self-surrender." [41]

Having yielded up his own identity to write his work, the Edwardian wished the reader to make comparable sacrifices. The *hypocrite lecteur* whom Baudelaire had arraigned was the reader who thought he might observe without joining in the work of art. This was to pass through the house like an irresponsible tenant, and the Edwardian novelist was too good a landlord for that. The reader must become responsible, must pay his rent. The sense of the importance of what their books were doing, the sense that only art, working through religious metaphor, can give life value, made the writers free to ask a great deal of their readers, and the literature of the time moved towards greater difficulty, the revival of Donne in 1912 being one of its manifestations, or towards greater importunacy, as in Lawrence. As Henry James remarked to a writer who complained that a meeting of authors was dull, "Hewlett, we are not here to enjoy ourselves."

It may seem that, though I have offered to exhibit two faces of Edward, I have in fact shown only one, and that one staring urgently toward the atomic age. Yet modern as Edwardian literature was, it was not fully modern. There was a difference in mood, which Yeats hinted at when he said that after 1900 nobody did any of the violent things they had done in the nineties. Can we not detect in this period, so distinguished in many ways, its writers so strict with themselves and with us, a sensible loss of vigor and heat? The Edwardians managed to retain much of the stability of the Victorians, but they did so only by becoming artful where their predecessors had seemed artless. The easy skill of Victorian narrative disappears, and while the Edwardians have good reasons for trying for more awesome effects, their work does not escape the charge of being self-conscious, almost *voulu*. It is the age of prefaces and of revisions. Their secular miracles, which they arranged so graciously, seem too easy now, and the modern equivalents of them, in Malamud's *The Assistant* or Bellow's *Henderson the Rain King* for example, are deliberately wrought with far greater restraint. Writers of social protest like Galsworthy seem, as Esmé Wingfield-Stratford points out, resigned to their own helplessness.[42] H. G. Wells, though so energetic, seems when he is not at his best too devout toward science, toward popular mechanics, and the later history of his writing of novels, which Gordon Ray has described, makes us wonder if even earlier he was quite so energetic as he appeared. Bennett presents his slices of life with the assurance of a good chef that life is appetizing, yet he has mastered his ingredients without much flair. *A Portrait of the Artist* is a work of genius, but wanting in gusto; and even Yeats is for much of this time more eloquent than implicated, not so much passionate as in favor of passion. Conrad achieves his effects, yet so laboriously, and with awkward narrators like Marlow who, in spite of his laudable artistic purposes, is a bit of a stick. The repetition of words and images, while helpful to the creation of unity, gives an air of pedantry to this aspiring period; the bird flies, but with leaden wings. I should like to find in George Gissing's book, *The Private Papers of Henry Ryecroft* (1903), a reflection of this diminution of vitality in a period that prided itself on its life. Gissing lived turbulently enough, but in this autobiographical fiction he is at pains to seem full of calm; a writer today might live calmly, but would want his books to be distraught.

The war, for I will not deny that it took place, made everything harder. The Edwardian confidence in artistic sensibility was broken down; the possibility of nothingness seems to replace the conviction of somethingness. Those Edwardian writers who lived through the war found stability less easy to come by. Before the war Yeats could write "The Magi," with its longing for violence; after the war he wrote "The Second Coming," in which violence inspires horror. Forster, who had accomplished his secular miracles rather handily in his early books, as by the trick of sending his thinner-blooded characters to lush Italy, descends lower to *A Passage to India,* where there is more brutality, and where the realizations to which he brings his personages are less ample, less reassuring. Pound, content with his troubadours before the war, turns upon himself in *Mauberley* with a strange blend of self-destruction and self-justification. Eliot, after politely mocking Edwardian politeness in "Prufrock," becomes impolite in *The Waste Land*. Lawrence becomes strident, frantic, exhortatory, almost suffocating his own mind. Virginia Woolf, unable to find herself before the war, discovers at last a tense point around which to organize her books, and this is not so much unity as the threat of the break-down of unity. Joyce, content to stay in the conscious mind in his earlier work, descends to a fiercer underworld in the *Circe* episode of *Ulysses,* where Edward VII appears, appropriately now turned to a nightmare figure babbling hysterically of "Peace, perfect peace." [43] The miracle of birth was accomplished in *A Portrait of the Artist* without much resistance, but the comparable miracle in *Ulysses,* Bloom's rescue of Stephen in a world where gratuitous kindness seems out of context, is described by Joyce with great circumspection, as if humanistic miracles now embarrassed him. The religion of life keeps most of its Edwardian adherents, but it has begun to stir up its own atheists and agnostics.

Notes

RUTH Z. TEMPLE
The Ivory Tower as Lighthouse

1. Had I the space to do so, I should be prepared to go further and to argue that the dominant criticism of our time—New Criticism—derives from aesthetic.

2. A much better reconsideration is *Great Victorians,* ed. by H. J. Massingham and Hugh Massingham (London, 1932).

3. The *Oxford Companion to English Literature* defines "Victorian" as: "an improved standard of decency and morality; a self-satisfaction engendered by the great increase of wealth, the prosperity of the nation as a whole, and the immense industrial and scientific development; conscious rectitude, and deficient sense of humor; an unquestioning acceptance of authority and orthodoxy." These recognizable characteristics of the age are not immediately recognizable as conducive to the making of great literature.

4. Wellek and Warren point out that "there is . . . no historical justification for the present usually accepted periods of English

literature. One cannot escape the conclusion that they constitute an indefensible jumble of political, literary and artistic labels." They argue that "The literary period should be established by purely literary criteria." *Theory of Literature* (New York, 1949), p. 277.

5. Esmé Wingfield-Stratford contends that the Victorian age should end about 1870 and the remaining years of the century be rechristened. "Elizabethan is not more different from Victorian than the atmosphere of the Great Exhibition from that of the Diamond Jubilee." *The Victorian Sunset* (London, 1932), p. v.

6. William Gaunt, *The Aesthetic Adventure* (New York [c. 1945]), p. 71.

7. E. Chandler, *Pater on Style* (Copenhagen, 1958).

8. Page 144. I quote Gaunt only to give a taste of his intellectual quality and style. Brooks and Wimsatt cite his *Aesthetic Adventure* as an authority on the period. *Literary Criticism: A Short History* (New York, 1957). It does not deserve this status. A much sounder book is Holbrook Jackson's *The Eighteen Nineties* (first published 1913, reissued in Pelican Books).

9. Written for *The Eighteen Eighties,* ed. by Walter De la Mare, reprinted in *Selected Essays, 1917–32* (New York [c. 1932]), pp. 354, 355.

10. *The Aesthetic of Walter Pater* (New York, 1940).

11. *The Writings of Walter Pater* (thesis; Bryn Mawr, Pa., 1933).

12. *Autobiographies* (London, 1956), p. 302.

13. *Prefaces and Essays* (London, 1933), p. 345 (from *The Bookman,* 1906).

14. Preface, *Studies in the History of the Renaissance.*

15. *Messages,* trans. by Montgomery Belgion (New York [c. 1927]), p. 291.

16. Even here, the impressionist criticism may not be so very far removed from the New Criticism. See Richard Forster's "Criticism as Poetry," *Criticism* (Spring, 1959), pp. 100–122.

17. "Two Symbolists," *Figures of Several Centuries* (London, 1916), p. 304.

18. Brooks and Wimsatt fall into this error.

19. "The Trembling of the Veil," in *Autobiographies,* p. 302.

20. *Ibid.,* p. 139.

21. Between 1881 and 1892 some 120 items in *Punch* referred to him. On the Continent his works fared even better than in England, and they have been widely translated. But there aestheticism is less likely to seem either laughable or wicked.

22. Malcolm Brown, *George Moore: a Reconsideration* (Univ. of Washington Press [c. 1955]), p. 98.

23. See his Introduction to *The Oxford Book of Modern Verse* (New York, 1936).

HELMUT E. GERBER
The Nineties: Beginning, End, or Transition?

1. *Oscar Wilde and the Yellow Nineties* (New York, 1940), p. 151.

2. *The Men of the Nineties* (London, 1920), p. 1.

3. *Modern English Literature* (New York, 1897), pp. 384–85.

4. *The Renaissance of the Nineties* (London, 1911), p. 16.

5. *The Beardsley Period* (London, 1925), Introduction and chap. I.

6. *The Eighteen Nineties* (London, 1913) and *John Lane and the Nineties* (London, 1936), respectively.

7. *"Attraverso il centenario di* G. B. Shaw *quello di* O. Wilde," *Nuova Antologia* (July, 1957), 377–86.

8. "The Existence of Symbolism," *Kenyon Review,* XIX (Summer, 1957), 425–47, trans. by Malcolm Cowley.

9. *The Eighteen Nineties,* p. 23.

10. "Literary Periods: Late Victorian, Post-Victorian, Early Modern, Transitional?" *English Fiction in Transition (1880–1920),* I (Fall–Winter, 1957), 4–6. This newsletter-journal of the MLA conference is published two or three times a year in the Department of English at Purdue University.

11. "Art and Shoddy," *Forum* (1893), reprinted in *Realities and Ideals* (New York, 1908).

12. *Le mouvement aesthétique et "décadent" en Angleterre: 1873–1900* (Paris, 1931), p. ii.

13. See, for example, the following: Granville Hicks, *Figures in Transition* (1939), especially the chapter on "The Changing Novel"; Harold Williams, *Outlines of Modern English Literature: 1890–1914* (1920), especially the chapters on "Poets of the Transition"; Abel Chevalley, *Le roman anglais de notre temps* (1921), especially chap. III, which begins with a section called *"Une période de transition";* Harry J. Marks, "The First Stage of the Cultural Crisis: The Pivotal Period in European History," *History of Ideas Newsletter,* IV (Jan., 1958), 2–6; T. M. Parrott and Willard Thorpe, eds., *Poetry of the Transition, 1850–1914* (1932).

14. "A Bookish Causerie," *Literary Review,* No. 60 (Winter, 1941), 114–20; *The Victorian Era* (Australia, 1938), p. 29; *Fifty*

Glorious Years of English Romantic Literature (Gravesend, 1947), p. 15; *The English Novel in Transition* (Norman, Oklahoma, 1942), p. 61.

15. In the Preface to *The Victorian Frame of Mind* (New Haven, 1957), Houghton says that attitudes "conspicuous from about 1830 to about 1870 . . . taken together and interrelated . . . provide a definition of Victorianism. . . . After 1870 . . . their dominance and their peculiar coherence was breaking down. Victorianism was dying, and a new frame of mind was emerging, a *late* Victorian frame of mind, which pointed to the postwar temper of the 1920s."

16. "Post-Victorian," *Cornhill Magazine* (May, 1944), p. 92, and *The Victorian Age in Literature* (London, 1913), p. 215, respectively.

17. The type of the attack made on the literature of the 1880s goes back at least to 1871, when Robert Buchanan's "The Fleshly School of Poetry" commented on the unhealthy sensuality of D. G. Rossetti's *Poems* (1870); to W. H. Mallock's *The New Republic* (1877); F. S. Burnand's *The Colonel* (1881); and, later, G. S. Street's *Autobiography of a Boy* (1894) and Robert Hichens's *The Green Carnation* (1894). However, it was Nordau's *Degeneration* (German, 1893; French, 1894; English, 1895) which stirred up the most furious battle. Among the replies to Nordau, between 1894 and 1897 alone, were Shaw's *The Sanity of Art,* A. E. Hake's *Regeneration,* and William Hirsch's *Genius and Degeneration.*

18. *Harper's New Monthly Magazine,* XXXVII (1893); in his *The Symbolist Movement* (London, rev. ed., 1908, 1911), Symons includes Verlaine among the symbolists. See B. Mor-

rissette, "Early English and American Critics of French Symbolism," in *Studies in Honor of Frederick W. Shipley* (St. Louis, 1942), pp. 159–80.

19. "The Aesthetic Revolt against Naturalism in Victorian Criticism," *PMLA,* LIII (Sept., 1938), 44–56.

20. "Symbolism," in *Axel's Castle* (New York, 1958), p. 25. The entire essay is significant for its bearing on the problem I review here.

21. Morrissette, "Early English and American Critics."

22. *The Romantic Nineties* (Garden City, N.Y., 1926), p. 269.

23. *Science and Society,* XXI (Summer, 1957), 210–21.

24. "Decadence in Modern Art" and "Art and Shoddy," both first published in *Forum* (1893), were reprinted in *Realities and Ideals* (New York, 1908). I quote from pp. 293, 295, 304, 306, 307, 308, 309, 310, and 318 of the latter volume. Clyde de L. Ryals, while defending the usefulness of the term "decadent" to describe a whole phase of the romantic movement current at the end of the nineteenth century, also writes that "if romanticism is the state which results when the classical synthesis has begun to disintegrate, then decadence is the result of the complete disintegration." "Toward a Definition of *Decadent* as applied to British Literature of the Nineteenth Century," *Journal of Aesthetics and Art Criticism,* XVII (Sept., 1958), 85–92.

25. For the succeeding quotations see the Boston edition (Small, Maynard, 1913), pp. 1, 29.

26. *Modern Philology,* XXX (1932), 124–28. Also see William Chislett, *The Classical Influence on English Literature in the Nineteenth Century* (Boston, 1928), and the chapter on Lionel

Johnson in Chislett's *Moderns and Near Moderns* (New York, 1928).

27. For the succeeding quotations see the London edition (A. Moring, 1913), pp. 16, 22.

28. *Journal of Aesthetics and Art Criticism,* XVI (March, 1958), 373–83.

29. "Writing 'Finis' to Decadence," *Independent,* LXXXIX (Jan. 15, 1917), 100.

30. *The Men of the Nineties,* pp. 134, 135, 136.

31. See H. Ausubel, *The Late Victorians* (Anvil Original, New York, 1955) and J. A. Rees, *The English Tradition: The Heritage of the Venturers* (London, 1934).

32. See also Maurice Baring, *Lost Lectures* (New York, 1932), chap. V, in which Baring, as an antidote to the usual view of the nineties, records the relative ordinariness of life in this decade.

33. *The Romantic Nineties* (Garden City, N.Y., 1926), p. 162; also pp. 207, 212, 213, 221–22, and 269.

34. John A. Lester, "Prose-Poetry Transmutations in the Poetry of John Davidson," *Modern Philology,* LVI (Aug., 1958), 38–44, shows a blending of traits in Davidson's work as prose journalism supplies materials for the poetry.

35. *Essays and Studies of the English Association, 1941,* XXVII (Oxford, 1942), 66–75.

36. John Wilcox, in "The Beginning of *l'art pour l'art,*" *Journal of Aesthetics and Art Criticism,* XI (1953), 360, points out that even in France before 1848 there is often confusion of "the emerging doctrine about art with bohemianism and with the Romantic movement, a mistake easily made because all three

lines of thought occurred at the same time and often together in the same individual."

37. *The Romantic Agony* (New York, Meridian Books, 1956), p. xvi.

38. *L'idée de l'art pour l'art dans la littérature anglaise pendant la période victorienne* (Paris, 1931).

39. "The New Realism," *Fortnightly Review* (May, 1916).

40. See David Hayman, *Joyce et Mallarmé* (Paris, 1956; 2 vols.), in which we learn that Joyce discovered Mallarmé around 1900 in the work of Symons and Huysmans.

41. Chapters I and II, especially p. 43.

42. For the interesting suggestion of a relationship between the present-day "angry young men" and Wells and Hardy, see John Holloway, "Tank in the Stalls: Notes on the 'School of Anger,'" *Hudson Review,* X (Autumn, 1957), 424–29.

43. Pages 9–10, 27.

44. "John Galsworthy: An Interpretation of Modernity," *Review of Reviews,* XLIII (May, 1911), 634–36, reprinted in *Is There Anything New Under the Sun?* (London, 1913), 183–200.

45. *Sources of Art Nouveau* (New York, 1956), trans. by Ragnar Christopherson.

46. "Emergent Modernism in Late Victorian Fiction," *South Atlantic Quarterly,* XLIV (1945), 286–93.

47. *Fifty Glorious Years of English Romantic Literature: 1870–1920* (Gravesend, 1947), p. 33.

48. *The Novel and the Modern World* (Chicago, 1939), chap. I, and *Poetry and the Modern World* (Chicago, 1940), chap. I, and p. 17.

49. *Journal of Aesthetics and Art Criticism,* XVI (March,

1958), 306–18. Also see Paul West, "A Note on the 1890s," *English,* XII (Summer, 1958), 54–57, which deals chiefly with artists but also speaks of the cultivation of "separateness."

50. Also see Vincent Brome, *Six Studies in Quarrelling* (London, 1958).

51. Samuel Chew, in his Pierpont Morgan Library address "The Web of English Culture," traces the note of melancholy from the Old English elegy "The Wanderer" to T. S. Eliot's "The Wasteland."

52. Rupert Hart-Davis is editing the collected letters of Wilde; Arthur C. Young is editing the Gissing-Bertz correspondence; Royal A. Gettmann is editing the Wells-Gissing correspondence; Anthony Curtis is preparing a new biography of Gissing; Edwin Gilcher has been working on a definitive bibliography of the works of George Moore; I have recently published an annotated bibliography of writings about George Moore, and I am presently preparing for publication some two hundred letters from Moore to T. Fisher Unwin; Charles Burkhart is editing some Moore-Gosse letters; Dowson's letters are, I am told, being edited; and more similar primary work is under way.

53. See T. E. M. Boll, "Walter Besant on the Art of the Novel," *English Fiction in Transition (1880–1920),* II (Spring, 1959), 28–35.

THOMAS R. WHITAKER
W. B. Yeats: History and the Shaping Joy

1. *Letters,* ed. by Allan Wade (New York, 1954), p. 402.
2. Yeats, *Plays and Controversies* (New York, 1924), p. v.

3. *Poems, 1899–1905* (London and Dublin, 1906), pp. xii–xiii.

4. Augusta Gregory, *Gods and Fighting Men* (London, 1904), pp. xx, xxi; *Samhain* (1908), pp. 8–9; Yeats, *Autobiography* (New York, 1953), pp. 304, 305.

5. *Essays* (New York, 1924), p. 392; *Autobiography,* p. 304.

6. *Plays and Controversies* (New York, 1924), pp. 99, 115.

7. *Works of Blake* ed. by E. J. Ellis and W. B. Yeats (London, 1893), I, 415, 357.

8. *Ibid.,* I, 273; Schopenhauer, *The World as Will and Idea,* trans. by Haldane & Kemp (London, 1896), I, 238, 347; Yeats, *Essays,* p. 337; Schopenhauer, I, 346, 265.

9. Yeats, *Autobiography,* pp. 164, 165; *Essays,* p. 315.

10. *Essays,* p. 316.   11. *Plays and Controversies,* p. 123.

12. *Letters,* p. 454.

13. See Gregory, *Gods and Fighting Men,* p. xx; Yeats, *Essays,* p. 267.

14. *Ulysses* (Modern Library ed.), p. 385.

15. See Yeats, *Pages from a Diary Written in 1930* (Dublin, 1944), p. 21.

16. *Essays,* pp. 418, 419–20, 376.

17. Thomas Parkinson, *W. B. Yeats: Self-Critic* (Berkeley, Calif., 1951), p. 108.

18. Yeats, *Essays,* pp. 14, 201, 138, 161, 172, 125.

19. *Plays and Controversies,* p. 113.

20. *Autobiography,* p. 314; *Essays,* pp. 395, 295–96.

21. *Essays,* p. 421; Blake, *Complete Writings,* ed. by Geoffrey Keynes (London, 1957), p. 613; Yeats, *Essays,* p. 384.

22. Jacob Boehme, *Six Theosophic Points and Other Writings,*

trans. by John Rolleston Earle (Ann Arbor, 1958), p. 175; "The Man Who Dreamed of Faeryland."

23. *Essays,* pp. 398, 255, 435–36; Patmore, *Principle in Art* (London, 1898), pp. 31–34, and *The Rod, the Root and the Flower* (London, 1950), p. 146.

24. See Yeats, *Autobiography,* p. 317.

25. *Essays,* p. 435; *Autobiography,* p. 125.

26. *Autobiography,* p. 304; *Essays,* p. 423.

27. *Essays,* pp. 83, 84. (The first statement is a quotation from *Queen Mab* III.174–75.)

GORDON RAY
H. G. Wells Tries to Be a Novelist

1. *Listener,* LIX (1958), 469.

2. *Experiment in Autobiography* (London, 1934), p. 623.

3. *Ibid.,* p. 418.   4. *Ibid.,* p. 310.

5. The writer is preparing an article on this subject.

6. "Popular Writers and Press Critics," *Saturday Review,* 8 February 1896, p. 145.

7. "Mr. Barrie's New Book," *Saturday Review,* 14 November 1896, p. 526.

8. "The Lost Stevenson," *Saturday Review,* 13 June 1896, p. 604.

9. *Works,* Atlantic Edition (28 vols.; London, 1924–27), XIII, 13. Hereafter cited as *Works.* Similarly in his ironical account of the popular author Sidney Revel in *Kipps,* Wells writes of " 'Red Hearts a-Beating,' the romance that had made him. It was a tale of spirited adventure, full of youth and beauty and naïve passion

and generous devotion, bold, as the *Bookman* said, and frank in places, but never in the slightest degree morbid." (*Works,* VIII, 256.) It may be noted that the vogue of the romance led to a profound popular misunderstanding of the purpose and significance of Conrad's work. In an age when it was said that "a story filled with tea fights is a novel, while if it is filled with sea fights it is a romance," his books were assimilated by an undiscriminating public to the yarns of such writers as W. Clark Russell. Hence Conrad's irritated insistence that he was not a "sea-novelist."

10. "The New American Novelists," *Saturday Review,* 5 September 1896, p. 262.

11. "Certain Critical Opinions," *Saturday Review,* 11 July 1896, p. 33.

12. *Saturday Review,* 30 May 1896, pp. 557–58.

13. "Fiction," *Saturday Review,* 22 February 1896, pp. 208–9. W. E. Henley thought this "the most brilliant [review] that has yet appeared in the *Saturday"* (manuscript letter from H. Blanchamp to Wells, 23 March 1896; University of Illinois Library).

14. "Joan Haste," *Saturday Review,* 21 September 1895, p. 386. With Lucas Cleeve's *Epicures* Wells was more abrupt. It was "malarial rubbish," he wrote, "which ought to be abated as a public nuisance." ("A Bad Novel," *Saturday Review,* 19 September 1896, pp. 318–19.)

15. "The Novels of Mr. George Gissing," *Contemporary Review,* LXXII (August, 1897), 195.

16. G. Jean-Aubry, *Joseph Conrad: Life and Letters* (2 vols.; New York, 1927), I, 259.

17. "Mr. Barrie's New Book," *Saturday Review*, 14 November 1896, p. 526.

18. "Fiction," *Saturday Review*, 7 December 1895, p. 769. In theory, if not in practice, Wells remained faithful to this conception of realism until the end of his life. We find him writing to Frank Swinnerton (photocopy of manuscript letter, Univ. of Illinois) on 17 May 1943: "The weakness of your book . . . is insufficient penetration into motives. A novel is as penetrating an inquiry into human behaviour and human life as [the] writer is capable of. *Why* do people behave like this, is our professional objective. But your motivation in this book is plot motivation."

19. "The Novels of Mr. George Gissing," *Contemporary Review*, LXXII (August, 1897), 193.

20. "The Novel of Types," *Saturday Review*, 4 January 1896, pp. 23–24.

21. "The Democratic Culture," *Saturday Review*, 13 March 1897, p. 273.

22. "Jude the Obscure," *Saturday Review*, 8 February 1896, p. 154.

23. "A Slum Novel," *Saturday Review*, 28 November 1896, p. 573.

24. "Mr. Grant Allen's New Novel," *Saturday Review*, Supplement, 14 December 1895, p. 786. The subtitle of *The British Barbarians* is "A Hill-top Novel."

25. "The Depressed School," *Saturday Review*, Supplement, 27 April 1895, p. 531. This matter is further developed in a letter which Wells wrote to Henley, 4 February 1900, about a visit he had made to a mortally afflicted friend: "He lies in bed and he

cannot talk and I'm damned if I see how it is going to go on. The thing has no point at all. It is one of those disastrous muddy affairs that you cannot take hold of anywhere. It makes me think there is something George Gissingish about Almighty God. It's grey and dismal & that's all the point it has." (Photocopy of manuscript letter, Univ. of Illinois.)

26. "Fiction," *Saturday Review,* 18 April 1896, p. 405. See also "The New American Novelists," 5 September 1896, pp. 262–63.

27. *Saturday Review,* 14 November 1896, p. 526.

28. "A Slum Novel," *Saturday Review,* 28 November 1896, p. 573.

29. "Margaret Ogilvy," *Saturday Review,* 23 January 1897, p. 94.

30. "An Outcast of the Islands," *Saturday Review,* 16 May 1896, pp. 509–10. Conrad took this criticism, which Wells went on to document in detail, very seriously.

31. "Three *Yellow-Book* Story-Tellers," *Saturday Review,* 1 June 1895, p. 731.

32. *Ibid.*

33. Conrad, *The Nigger of the "Narcissus,"* in *Works* (20 vols.; London, 1921–27), III, xi.

34. Typescript of preface to Russian translation of his selected works (Univ. of Illinois), a revision of which was published as "Mr. Wells Explains Himself," *T.P.'s Magazine* (December, 1911).

35. Undated manuscript letter (Univ. of Illinois).

36. See "The Well at the World's End," *Saturday Review,* 17 October 1896, p. 413.

37. *Experiment in Autobiography,* p. 179.

38. Typescript of preface to Russian translation of his selected works (Univ. of Illinois).

39. *Experiment in Autobiography,* p. 375.

40. *Saturday Review,* 13 April 1895, p. 475.

41. *Works,* VII, ix.

42. *Experiment in Autobiography,* p. 207.

43. *Fabian Essays in Socialism* (London, 1889), p. 29. Wells's *Saturday* reviews are particularly revealing in this connection. In these unsigned articles for Harris's unconventional journal he had no need to be on guard regarding unacceptable biases, as he did later writing over his own name. See particularly "Jude the Obscure," 8 February 1896, pp. 153–54; "Side Talks with Girls," 14 March 1896, pp. 281–82; "The Making of Men at Cambridge," 13 February 1897, pp. 174–75; and "The Democratic Culture," 13 March 1897, pp. 273–74.

44. *Works,* XII, 241.

45. This distinction has Wells's sanction. In an autobiographical sketch contributed to *The Royal College of Science Magazine,* XV (April, 1903), 203, he noted: "Mr. Wells has written one novel."

46. Photocopy of manuscript letter, 5 September 1895 (Univ. of Illinois).

47. Manuscript letter, 25 November [1897] (Univ. of Illinois).

48. Photocopy of manuscript letter, October, 1898 (Univ. of Illinois).

49. Photocopy of manuscript letter, 10 December 1898 (Univ. of Illinois).

50. Photocopy of manuscript letter, 15 June 1900 (Univ. of Illinois).

51. Photocopy of undated manuscript letter [1901] (Univ. of Illinois).

52. In the possession of the writer.

53. Manuscript letter to Elizabeth Bruce, 22 June 1900 (Univ. of Illinois).

54. *Ibid.*   55. At the University of Illinois.

56. *Works,* VII, 242–43.   57. *Ibid.,* VII, 340.

58. *Ibid.,* VII, 516–17. Earlier in the novel Chaffery in his role of *raisonneur* had anticipated these views (*ibid.* VII, 477).

59. See, for example, *ibid.,* VII, 303–4.

60. *Ibid.,* VII, 415–20.

61. Early manuscript draft of the final chapter (Univ. of Illinois).

62. A subject that fascinated Wells, as is testified, for example, by "Apparitions and Thought-Transference," *Saturday Review,* 20 October 1894, pp. 435–36.

63. *Works,* VII, 314, 290, 304, 400.   64. *Ibid.,* VII, ix.

65. Geoffrey West, *H. G. Wells* (New York, 1930), p. 120.

66. Photocopy of manuscript letter to Pinker, October, 1898 (Univ. of Illinois).

67. See *Works,* VIII, ix.

68. Unpublished manuscript of 1944 entitled "Exasperations" (Univ. of Illinois).

69. "Two Novels," 27 June 1896, p. 653.

70. *Works,* VIII, 375.

71. Manuscript letter, Bennett to Wells, 9 November 1905 (Univ. of Illinois).

72. *Works,* VIII, 306–14. Wells is at pains to make Kipps

disown Masterman's views (315, 366), a device that does not mis-lead the acute.

73. *Works*, VIII, 44, 50–51.

74. *Ibid.*, VIII, 161, 168, 259, 287.   75. *Ibid.*, VIII, 232.

76. *Henry James and H. G. Wells*, ed. by Leon Edel and Gordon N. Ray (Urbana, 1958), p. 105.

77. *Works*, XII, 415–16.

78. Photocopy of manuscript letter, 4 December 1898 (Univ. of Illinois).

79. Manuscript letter, 9 November 1905 (Univ. of Illinois).

80. *Works*, VIII, 21, 128, 187.   81. *Ibid.*, VIII, 329–32.

82. Typescript (Univ. of Illinois).   83. *Works*, XII, ix.

84. *Ibid.*, XII, 215.   85. *Ibid.*, XII, 26, 200, 182.

86. *Ibid.*, XII, 181.   87. *Ibid.*, XII, 198, 202, 308.

88. *Ibid.*, XII, 366, 329.

89. Wells took some of the details of Ponderevo's business ventures and later manner of life from the career of the notorious Whitaker Wright, a mining company promoter who was tried for fraud in 1904 and shortly afterwards committed suicide. See particularly the highly colored reminiscences of Wright by a close associate, Roland Belfort, in "A Tale of a City Crisis," *Nineteenth Century*, CVI (November, 1929), 699–709. West (*H. G. Wells*, p. 156) suggests that Wright's death may have been Wells's starting point for *Tono-Bungay*. Ponderevo is made to refer to Wright at one point in the novel (*Works*, XII, 476).

90. *Works*, XII, 283, 351.   91. *Ibid.*, XII, 300, 447.

92. *Ibid.*, XII, 507, 11, 18–19.

93. *Ibid.*, XII, 347, 519–20, 297, 447.   94. *Ibid.*, XII, 528–29.

95. Manuscript of *Tono-Bungay* (Univ. of Illinois).

96. *Works*, XII, ix.

97. *Experiment in Autobiography*, pp. 103, 104, 134, 147, 196–197.

98. The point of transition from the first to the second is *Works*, XVII, 164.

99. *Ibid.*, XVII, 3.   100. *Ibid.*, XVII, 12–14.

101. *Ibid.*, XVII, 280, 12, 21, 61, 90, 102–3, 255, 44, 50, 57.

102. *Ibid.*, 32, 44, 117, 134.   103. *Ibid.*, XVII, 212.

104. *Ibid.*, XVII, 219–21.   105. *Ibid.*, XVII, 228–30.

106. *Ibid.*, XVII, 240–41.   107. *Ibid.*, XVII 246, 278–80.

108. *Ibid.*, XVII, 161–64 (the only significant instance of auctorial intervention).

109. *The History of Mr. Polly* (London, 1947), p. vi.

110. See his preface to *The History of Mr. Polly* (New York, 1941).

111. *Works*, XVII, ix.

112. Typescript of preface to Russian translation of Wells's selected works (Univ. of Illinois).

113. "My Lucky Moment," *The View*, 29 April 1911, p. 212.

114. "Peep at the Future," *Evening Standard and St. James's Gazette*, 2 January 1911, p. 9.

115. "My Lucky Moment."

116. *Experiment in Autobiography*, p. 325.

117. *Works*, VIII, 94.

118. *Henry James and H. G. Wells*, p. 164.   119. *Ibid.*, p. 28.

120. "H. G. Wells Writes His Own Obituary," *Listener*, XVI (15 July 1936), 98.

121. *The History of Mr. Polly*, p. viii.

122. *Experiment in Autobiography,* pp. 499–500.

123. *An Assessment of Twentieth Century Literature* (London, 1951), p. 21.

GERALD WEALES
The Edwardian Theater and the Shadow of Shaw

1. See Granville Barker, "The Theatre: The Next Phase," *English Review,* V (July, 1910), 631–48.

2. *Ibid.* See also the essays in *The Dramatic Works of St. John Hankin,* Vol. III (London, 1912). "Puritanism and the English Stage" (pp. 131–48) appeared first in *Fortnightly Review,* December, 1906; "How to Run an Art Theatre for London" (pp. 171–79), in November, 1907; and "The Need for an Endowed Theatre" (pp. 203–21), in December, 1908. See also John Galsworthy, "Some Platitudes Concerning Drama," *Fortnightly Review,* LXXXVI N.S. (December, 1909), 1004–10.

3. "Some Platitudes Concerning Drama," in *The Inn of Tranquility* (New York, 1928), p. 199. The essay as it appears in this volume is a restrained version of the original one in the *Fortnightly Review.*

4. "The Author's Apology," *Our Theatre in the Nineties,* Vol. I (London, 1932). Preface originally written for the 1906 *Dramatic Opinions and Essays.*

5. *The Inn of Tranquility,* p. 199.

6. *Bernard Shaw and Mrs. Patrick Campbell, Their Correspondence,* ed. by Alan Dent (New York, 1952), p. 180. Letter dated November 4, 1914.

7. *The Inn of Tranquility,* p. 189.

8. *The Dramatic Works of St. John Hankin,* III, 127.

9. "J. M. Barrie as a Dramatist," *The Bookman,* XXXIX (October, 1910), 13–21.

10. See Gerald Weales, "The Poet As Player," *New World Writing,* No. 11 (New York, 1957), p. 236.

11. E. Bradlee Watson and Benfield Pressey have both *Justice* and *Loyalties* in *Contemporary Drama* (New York, 1941), but in their shorter, paperback collections, *Contemporary Drama, 11 Plays* (1956) and *Contemporary Drama, 15 Plays* (1959), Galsworthy has disappeared.

12. *The Dramatic Works of St. John Hankin,* III, 168.

13. Vladimir Nabokov, *Lolita* (New York, 1958), p. 156.

14. *Bernard Shaw's Letters to Granville Barker,* ed. by C. B. Purdom (London, 1956), p. 7.

15. C. B. Purdom, *Harley Granville Barker* (Cambridge, Mass., 1956), p. 290. Purdom, an Englishman, of course does not use the American word *director.* Appendix II (pp. 290–92) lists Barker's directorial credits.

16. Quoted in *Harley Granville Barker,* p. 15. The review is dated January 28, 1901.

17. *Bernard Shaw's Letters to Granville Barker,* p. 115. Letter dated January 19, 1908.

18. *Harley Granville Barker,* p. 205.

RICHARD ELLMANN
Two Faces of Edward

1. Virginia Woolf, *Mr. Bennett and Mrs. Brown* (London, The Hogarth Essays, 1924), p. 4.

2. Esmé Wingfield-Stratford, *The Victorian Aftermath* (New York, 1934), p. 2.

3. Lascelles Abercrombie, "Literature," in *Edwardian England,* ed. by F. J. C. Hearnshaw (London, 1933), pp. 185–203.

4. W. B. Yeats, Introduction to *The Oxford Book of Modern Verse* (Oxford, 1936), p. xi.

5. James Joyce, *A Portrait of the Artist as a Young Man,* in *The Portable James Joyce,* ed. by Harry Levin (New York, 1949), p. 432.

6. H. Granville-Barker, *Three Plays* (New York, 1909), p. 271.

7. D. H. Lawrence, *The Rainbow* (New York, Modern Library), p. 87.

8. H. G. Wells, *Experiment in Autobiography* (New York, 1934), pp. 573–78.

9. James Joyce, *A Portrait of the Artist as a Young Man,* in *The Portable James Joyce,* p. 488.

10. Granville-Barker, *Three Plays,* p. 252.

11. Marcel Proust, *Le Temps retrouvé,* p. 16 (Volume VII in *Oeuvres Complètes;* Paris, 1932); cf. *Remembrance of Things Past* (New York, Modern Library Giant), II, 996.

12. E. M. Forster, *Where Angels Fear to Tread* (New York, 1950), p. 267.

13. Forster, *The Longest Journey* (Norfolk, Conn., n.d.), p. 327.

14. Forster, *A Room with a View* (Norfolk, Conn., n.d.), p. 204.

15. *Ibid.,* p. 310.

16. Granville-Barker, *Three Plays,* p. 250.

17. Joyce, "The Dead," in *The Portable James Joyce,* p. 238.

18. H. G. Wells, *Tono-Bungay* (London, Penguin Books, 1946), p. 10.

19. Henry James, *The Ambassadors* (New York, Harper, 1948), p. 150.

20. Joyce, *Portrait of the Artist,* p. 525.

21. Quoted by Harry T. Moore in *The Intelligent Heart* (New York, 1954), p. 191.

22. Ford Madox Ford, *Collected Poems* (London, 1914), p. 17.

23. Joseph Conrad, *Conrad's Prefaces,* ed. by Edward Garnett (London, 1937), p. 173.

24. Wells, *Tono-Bungay,* p. 377.

25. Letter from G. Bernard Shaw to James, Jan. 17, 1909 in Henry James, *The Complete Plays,* ed. by Leon Edel (New York, 1949), p. 643.

26. Quoted by Ford Madox Ford in *The English Novel* (Philadelphia, 1929), p. 147.

27. *The Critical Writings of James Joyce,* ed. by Ellsworth Mason and Richard Ellmann (New York, 1959), p. 40.

28. Wells, *Experiment in Autobiography,* p. 619.

29. Yeats, *A Vision* (New York, 1938), p. 25.

30. Woolf, "Modern Fiction," in *The Common Reader* (London, 1925), p. 189.

31. Ford, *The English Novel,* p. 147.

32. Quoted by Walter B. Rideout in "Edith Wharton's *The House of Mirth,*" in *Twelve Original Essays on Great American Novels,* ed. by Charles Shapiro (Detroit, 1958), p. 151.

33. *Conrad's Prefaces,* p. 49.

34. The title of Frederick Baron Corvo's novel, written in 1909.

35. Wells, *Boon* (New York, 1915), p. 106.

36. *Ibid.*, p. 109.

37. Wells, *Experiment in Autobiography*, pp. 527–28.

38. T. E. Hulme, *Speculations*, ed. by Herbert Read (London, 1949), pp. 180–81, 213.

39. Henry James, "Preface to 'The Golden Bowl,'" in *The Art of the Novel*, ed. by R. P. Blackmur (New York, 1950), p. 328.

40. Ezra Pound, *Gaudier-Brzeska* (London, 1916), p. 106.

41. *Conrad's Prefaces*, p. 110.

42. *The Victorian Aftermath*, p. 173.

43. Joyce, *Ulysses* (New York, Modern Library Giant, 1934), p. 575.

Supervising Committee, The English Institute, 1959

The Program

September 8 through September 11, 1959
CONFERENCES

I. *Issues in Current Medieval Literary Studies*
Directed by MORTON W. BLOOMFIELD, Ohio State University

   1. *Medieval Literary Theory*
      CRAIG LA DRIÈRE, Catholic University

   2. *Intellectual History in Literature*
      RICHARD H. GREEN, Johns Hopkins University

   3. *Linguistics*
      W. NELSON FRANCIS, Franklin and Marshall College

   4. *Folklore, Myth, and Ritual*
      FRANCIS L. UTLEY, Ohio State University

II. *The Edwardians: A Reappraisal*
Directed by RICHARD ELLMANN, Northwestern University

   1. *H. G. Wells Tries to Be a Novelist*
      GORDON N. RAY, University of Illinois

2. *W. B. Yeats: History and the "Shaping Joy"*
THOMAS R. WHITAKER, Oberlin College

3. *The Edwardian Theater and the Shadow of Shaw*
GERALD WEALES, University of Pennsylvania

4. *Two Faces of Edward*
RICHARD ELLMANN, Northwestern University

III. *Spenser's Faerie Queene: Revaluations*
Directed by HUGH N. MACLEAN, University of Cincinnati

1. *Spenser in the Tradition of Allegory*
A. C. HAMILTON, University of Washington

2. *The Myth of Florimell and Marinell*
WILLIAM BLISSETT, University of Saskatchewan

3. *The Poetic Prospect: From Vision to Process in the*
FAERIE QUEEN
HARRY BERGER, JR., Yale University

IV. *Source Study: A Critique*
Directed by CHARLES T. DAVIS, Princeton University

1. *Chaucer's Use of Dante*
HOWARD H. SCHLESS, Columbia University

2. *Myth, Method, and Shakespeare*
HERBERT WEISINGER, Michigan State University

3. *E. A. Robinson and Arthurian Romance*
CHARLES T. DAVIS, Princeton University

Registrants, 1959

Meyer Howard Abrams, Cornell University; Gellert Spencer Alleman, Newark College of Arts and Sciences, Rutgers University; Paul J. Alpers, Harvard University; Richard D. Altick, Ohio State University; Reta Anderson, Woman's College, University of North Carolina; Joseph Albert Appleyard, s.j., Harvard University; Mother Thomas Aquinas, o.s.u., College of New Rochelle; Robert W. Ayers, Georgetown University.

Sister Anne Barbara, Emmanuel College; Isabel Harriss Barr; Mary Prentice Barrows, University of California; Sister Marie of the Trinity Barry, Emmanuel College; Lynn C. Bartlett, Vassar College; Phyllis Bartlett, Queens College; Martin Carey Battestin, Wesleyan University; David W. Becker, Miami University; Frances Harriet Bennett, Ohio Northern University; Alice R. Bensen, Eastern Michigan University; Harry J. Berger, Yale University; Siegmund A. E. Betz, Our Lady of Cincinnati College; Whitney Blake; William Blissett, University of Saskatchewan; Morton W. Bloomfield, Ohio State University; Philip Bordinat, Miami University; James D. Boulger, Yale University; Muriel Bowden, Hunter College; Brother Clementian Francis Bowers, f.s.c., De La Salle College; the Reverend John Dominic Boyd, s.j., Bellarmine College; Leicester Bradner, Brown University; Mary Campbell Brill, West Virginia Wesleyan College; Reuben A. Brower, Harvard University; Margaret Bryant, Brooklyn College; Mrs. W. Bryher, Vaud, Switzerland; Jean R. Buchert, Woman's College, University of North Carolina; Brother Fidelian Burke, f.s.c., La Salle College; Arthur Burkhard; Katherine Burton, Wheaton College; Mary D. Bush, Woman's College, University of North Carolina.

Herbert Cahoon, Pierpont Morgan Library; Grace J. Calder, Hunter College; Elizabeth Cameron; Kenneth Cameron, Carl H. Pforzheimer Library; George Carr Camp, Southern Illinois University; Mother Angela Carson, o.s.u., College of New Rochelle; Mother Marie-Louise Casey, o.s.u., College of New Rochelle; Robert L. Chapman, Wilkes College; Hugh C. G. Chase; Sister Maryanna Childs, o.p., College of St. Mary of the Springs; Sister Mary Chrysostom, College of Mount Saint Vincent; Mother Madeleine Clary, o.s.u., College of New Rochelle; John Conley, John Carroll University; Francis X. Connolly, Fordham University; Marjorie D. Coogan, Brooklyn College; Allen Blow Cook, United States Naval Academy; John S. Coolidge, Swarthmore College; Joan Corbett, University of Richmond; David K. Cornelius; Roberta D. Cornelius, Randolph-Macon Woman's College; Francis Xavier Corrigan, Good Counsel College; Paul Cortissoz, Manhattan College; William R. Coulter, Roanoke College; G. Armour Craig, Amherst College; Martha Craig, Wellesley College; Lucille Crighton, Gulf Park College.

Elizabeth Adams Daniels, Vassar College; Arthur P. Davis,

Howard University; Charles Davis, Princeton University; Richard Beale Davis, University of Tennessee; Walter R. Davis, Williams College; Robert Adams Day, Queens College; Sara DeFord, Goucher College; Robert M. Dell, Pace College; Sister Mary Denise, R.S.M., College Misericordia; Charlotte D'Evelyn, Mount Holyoke College; Stewart Dodge, State Teachers College, Cortland, N.Y.; Sister Rose Bernard Donna, C.S.J., College of Saint Rose; Agnes M. Donohue, Barat College; Mother Mary Dowd, O.S.U., College of New Rochelle; Elizabeth Drew, Smith College; Edgar H. Duncan, Vanderbilt University; Ivar Lou Duncan, Belmont College; E. Catherine Dunn, The Catholic University of America; Mother Margaret Mary Dunn, Manhattanville College of the Sacred Heart.

Edward R. Easton, Pace College; Ursula Elizabeth Eder, Brooklyn College; Richard Ellmann, Northwestern University; Martha England, Queens College; David V. Erdman, New York Public Library; Sister Mary Estelle, O.P., Albertus Magnus College.

Alice Farrison, North Carolina College at Durham; W. Edward Farrison, North Carolina College at Durham; Arthur Fenner, Jr., University of Notre Dame; Edward G. Fletcher, University of Texas; F. Cudworth Flint, Dartmouth College; Claude R. Flory, Florida State University; Ephim G. Fogel, Cornell University; French Fogle, Claremont College; Stephen Fogle, University of Florida; George H. Ford, University of Rochester; Sister Mary Francis, College of Mount Saint Vincent; W. Nelson Francis, Franklin and Marshall College; Lewis Freese, Purdue University; Northrop Frye, Victoria College, University of Toronto.

Ligeia Gallagher, Loyola University; Helmut E. Gerber, Purdue University; Helen T. Greany, Columbia University; Richard Green, Johns Hopkins University.

A. C. Hamilton, University of Washington; Katharine Harris, Queens College; John A. Hart, Carnegie Institute of Technology; Allen T. Hazen, Columbia University; Thelma Henner, Queens College; the Reverend William B. Hill, s.j., Novitiate of St. Isaac Jogues; C. Fenno Hoffman, Jr., Massachusetts Institute of Technology; Norman N. Holland, Massachusetts Institute of Technology; C. Carroll Hollis, University of Detroit; Lillian Hornstein, New York University; Muriel J. Hughes, University of Vermont; Julia Hysham, Skidmore College.

Sister Mary Immaculate, o.p.; Robert S. Jackson, Yale University; Eleanor Jared, Huron College, University of Western Ontario; Sister Mary Joannes, r.s.m., Mercy College; S. F. Johnson, Columbia University; Iva Jones, Morgan State College.

Robert E. Kaske, University of North Carolina; Julian B. Kaye, Brooklyn College; John E. Keating, Kent State University; Alfred L. Kellogg, Rutgers University; Rev. Edward Kelly, s.j., Fordham University; Norman Kelvin, University College, Rutgers University; John P. Kirby, Randolph-Macon Woman's College; Rudolph Kirk, Rutgers University; Herbert L. Kleinfield, Temple University; Jacob Korg, University of Washington; Frank A. Krutzke, Colorado College.

James Craig La Drière, The Catholic University of America; Rev. John P. Lahey, s.j., Le Moyne College; Seymour Lainoff, Yeshiva College; the Reverend Henry St. C. Lavin, s.j., Loyola College, Baltimore; Lewis Leary, Columbia University; Jean S. Lindsay, Hunter College; Louis Locke, Madison College; W.

B. Long, Princeton University; Laura Hibbard Loomis; Roger Sherman Loomis, Columbia University; George deForest Lord, Yale University; Joseph P. Lovering, Canisius College; Winslow H. Loveland, Boston University; Edward Lowry, Mary Washington College of the University of Virginia; Eva Lüders, The Catholic University of America.

Charles J. McCann, Canisius College; John McChesney, Hotchkiss School; Thomas E. McCrory, University of Detroit; Robert M. MacGregor; Julia McGrew, Vassar College; Richard Macksey, The Johns Hopkins University; Hugh N. Maclean, University of Cincinnati; Rev. Terence McVeigh, s.j., Fordham University; Mother C. E. Maguire, r.s.c.j., Newton College of the Sacred Heart; Sister Elizabeth Marian, College of Mount Saint Vincent; Sister Julia Marie, College of Mount Saint Vincent; Mary H. Marshall, Syracuse University; Thomas F. Marshall, Kent State University; Harold C. Martin, Harvard University; Louis L. Martz, Yale University; Dorothy Mateer, College of Wooster; Harrison Neserold, Pennsylvania State University; Dorothy S. Milton, Ferris Institute; Francis E. Mineka, Cornell University; Sister Jeanne Pierre Mittnight, c.s.j., College of Saint Rose; Mother Grace Monahan, o.s.u., College of New Rochelle; J. Mitchell Morse, Pennsylvania State University.

Kerby Neill, The Catholic University of America; William Nelson, Columbia University; Helaine Newstead, Hunter College; John W. Nichol, Denison University; Eleanor Nicholes, Carl H. Pforzheimer Library; the Reverend William T. Noon, s.j., Fordham University; Sister M. Norma, o.p., Albertus Magnus College.

W. H. Sterg O'Dell, Drexel Institute of Technology; Mother

E. O'Gorman, Manhattanville College of the Sacred Heart; Sterling P. Olmsted, Rensselaer Polytechnic Institute; the Reverend Joseph E. O'Neill, s.j., Fordham University; the Reverend Walter J. Ong, s.j., St. Louis University; Ants Oras, University of Florida; James M. Osborn, Yale University; Charles A. Owen, University of Connecticut.

Coleman O. Parsons, The City College, New York; Norman Holmes Pearson, Yale University; Harry William Pedicord; Margaret I. Pfau, Elmira College; Rafael Alan Pollock, University of Notre Dame; Abbie Findlay Potts, Rockford College; George Foster Provost, Duquesne University; Max Putzel, University of Connecticut (Hartford); Richard E. Quaintance, Jr., Duke University; the Reverend Charles J. Quirk, s.j., Loyola University of the South.

Isabel Elizabeth Rathborne, Hunter College; Charles Arthur Ray, North Carolina College at Durham; Gordon N. Ray, University of Illinois; Sister Mary Raynelda, c.s.s.p., Madonna College; Allen Walker Read, Columbia University; Mrs. John H. Reed, Ohio Wesleyan University; Sister Catherine Regina, College of Mount Saint Vincent; Catherine M. Reigart, Brooklyn College; Warner G. Rice, University of Michigan; R. P. apRoberts, New York University; David Allan Robertson, Jr., Barnard College; Gerrit H. Roelofs, Kenyon College; Doris A. Russell, Vassar College.

Judith E. Scherer, Cornell University; Helene B. M. Schnabel; Howard H. Schless, Columbia University; Richard J. Schoeck, University of Notre Dame; Robert E. Scholes, University of Virginia; Flora Rheta Schreiber, The New School for Social Research; Aurelia G. Scott, Wagner College; Helen M. Scurr,

University of Bridgeport; Daniel Seltzer, Harvard University; Frank Eugene Seward, The Catholic University of America; F. Parvin Sharpless, Drexel Institute of Technology; John T. Shawcross, Newark College of Engineering; William Sloane, Dickinson College; J. Gordon Spaulding, University of British Columbia; George Stade, Columbia University; Nathan Comfort Starr, University of Florida; Jess Stein; David L. Stevenson, Western Reserve University; Keith Stewart, University of Cincinnati; Barbara Swain, Vassar College; the Reverend Paul Joel Sweeney, s.j., Xavier University.

Anne Robb Taylor, Connecticut College; Ruth Zabriskie Temple, Brooklyn College; H. Barton Thomas, Graham-Eckes School; Doris Stevens Thompson, Russell Sage College; Rosemond Tuve, Connecticut College; Dale Underwood, University of New Hampshire; Francis Lee Utley, Ohio State University; David M. Vieth, University of Kansas; Howard P. Vincent, Illinois Institute of Technology; Sister M. Vincentia, Albertus Magnus College; the Reverend Vianney F. Vormwald, o.f.m., Siena College.

Richard Waidelich, Goucher College; Eugene M. Waith, Yale University; Andrew J. Walker, Georgia Institute of Technology; Chad Walsh, Beloit College; Francis W. Warlow, Dickinson College; Gerald Weales, University of Pennsylvania; Dr. James J. Wey, University of Detroit; Herbert Weisinger, Michigan State University; Jeanne K. Welcher, St. John's University; Thomas R. Whitaker, Oberlin College; Mother Elizabeth White, r.s.c.j., Newton College of the Sacred Heart; John W. Wieler, Hunter College; Brother Joseph Wiesenfarth, f.s.c., De La Salle College; Dorothy Willis, Yale University; Matthew W. Wise,

Roanoke College; Ross G. Woodman, University of Western Ontario; Daniel H. Woodward, Mary Washington College; Philip S. Yedinsky, Drexel Institute of Technology; Philip Young, Pennsylvania State University; John A. Yunck, Michigan State University; Alex Zwerdling, Swarthmore College.

Acknowledgments

Permission to quote from the poetry of William Butler Yeats has been granted by The Macmillan Company, New York, and by A. P. Watt and Sons, London, for the following: various quotations from *Collected Poems* (Macmillan, 1956); *The King's Threshold* and *At the Hawk's Well,* in *Collected Plays* (Macmillan, 1953); the 1894 version of "Red Hanrahan's Song about Ireland," as given in the *Variorum Edition of the Poems* (Macmillan, 1957); and quotations from *The Shadowy Waters* as given in the *Letters,* edited by Allan Wade (Macmillan, 1955).